May the gems of wisdom and stories in JUST PLAIN SENSE bring to mind the gems of wisdom and stories you have discovered along your own lifes path.

Safe & Blessed Travels,

Jack A Ottoson

jackottoson@
AOL.Com

Just Plain Sense

Reflections of a Plains Pastor

Jack A. Ottoson, M.Div.

WESTBOW
PRESS®
A DIVISION OF THOMAS NELSON
& ZONDERVAN

WestBow Press books may be ordered through booksellers or by contacting:

WestBow Press
A Division of Thomas Nelson & Zondervan
1663 Liberty Drive
Bloomington, IN 47403
www.westbowpress.com
1 (866) 928-1240

ISBN: 978-1-5127-2286-4 (sc)
ISBN: 978-1-5127-2287-1 (e)

Library of Congress Control Number: 2015920349

Print information available on the last page.

WestBow Press rev. date: 4/1/2016

Contents

Acknowledgements.......................................vii
Testimonials ix
Foreword xi

Chapter 1 1
Chapter 2...25
Chapter 3...47
Chapter 4...71
Chapter 5...113
Chapter 6...134
Chapter 7...158

Postscript.. 209
Endnotes 211

Acknowledgements

First and foremost I want to thank my wife, Kathy Ottoson, for being the primary editor of <u>Just Plain Sense</u>. Kathy is my wife, my best friend and my faithful companion on life's journey. Our journey began as I dated "the girl next door" in 1967. Today a sign hanging on our front door says it all. "A fisherman lives here with the best catch of his life."

Over the past two years of rewriting and editing <u>Just Plain Sense,</u> I have been privileged to have dozens of friends read and offer suggestions for this book. Special thanks go to Terra Brock, Nathan & Erin Ottoson, Catherine Butler, Joe & Barbara Cameron, Jenee & John Castellanos, Rev. Dr. Marcia Cox, Sherryl Danks, Pastor Sean Garner, Nancy Gary, Tom Gemmer, Judi Gentile, Eleanor Sostarich, Dr. Audrey & Bob Hains, Tom & Elaine Hann, Per Olov & Eva Hansson, Rev. Zach Harris, Rev. Dr. Mel Jacob, Dr. Mary Jacob, Jean Kaczmarek, Keith & Teresa Kaczmarek, Curt Knapp, Rev. Jeff Linman, Sandy Marino, Maxine Merrill, Lynn & Rosa Moist, Mikael Ojdal, Craig & Gail Peterson, Ivy Piche, Rev. Paul Pollock, Camilla Porshede Johansson, Carol Riley, Veronica Vejsholt, Eddie & Laura Smallwood, Jim & Judy Smith, Susan Thompson, Harlan Tipton, Anne Vandewalle, Dr.

Sue Tipton, Linda Waugh, Gail O'Leary, John Wilson, MaryJo Mercier, Ove & Agneta Johansson, John & Yanni Plate, JoJean Brandl, Rev. Dr. Jim Mikkelson, Linda McNeill, John Peterson, Robert Rockett, Maryellen Wynn, Rev. Peter Rogness, Bishop Robert Schaefer, Rev. Jim Smith, Dr. Lon Arneson, Gene & Jackie Cody, J. B. Caldwell, Rev. Ron & Wahneeta Ryckman, Mel Lindauer, Tom Tharp, Rev. Bob Anderson, Rev. Charles Weinrich, Dr. Dan & Julie Good and Bill Good.

Thank you one and all for your time and support.

Testimonials

The stories that Jack captured in <u>Just Plain Sense</u> were very relevant. As the current President of our Church Council, I used several thoughts from this book for members to ponder prior to setting upon the business of the meeting. One particular one referred to sitting in a boat and the reason to move the boat out into the deeper water - to venture out beyond the familiarity of the shore. Easy and enjoyable reading.
Audrey Hains, Ph. D. in Educational Administration. School Administrator

<u>Just Plain Sense</u> appears to be a book written by a Lutheran Pastor. However, it is not just a book. It is a journey. It is a lifetime of wisdom laid bare and filled with gems mined from a lifetime of service and reflection. It is not about being a Lutheran, but it does tell a lot about being a Christian. It is not about being a pastor, but it tells a lot about being a human being. For as deep as the meaning is within the many everyday stories, it is less a sermon by Pastor Jack, and more of a conversation with Captain Jack on his fishing boat. My advice: drop your line in the water and sit a while. You will be amazed at what you might catch!"

Pastor Zach Harris, M.Div., Ascension Lutheran Church, Wilson, N.C.

Just Plain Sense is a heartfelt and honest testimonial of personal life lessons and life stories that is as touching as it is comical! Jack Ottoson has a humbling way of incorporating his own experiences into each chapter. Just Plain Sense is thought provoking and can be described as a "feel good book."

Terra Brock, MSM, Masters in Management, Associate Director-University Admissions

Jack's writing style made me laugh and cry all in the same chapter. If one of his stories doesn't remind you of your own life stories...maybe you aren't paying attention.

Tom Hann, B.S. in agriculture. Farmer, realtor, entrepreneur.

I have never been an avid reader but the stories in Just Plain Sense captured my attention immediately. Jack has a way of writing that is both easy reading and draws you in. The chapters help you ponder your own life's adventures and the questions at the end of each chapter are both fun and thought provoking.

Elaine Hann, M.S. Ed., Masters in Education. Teacher and Principal

Foreword

I suppose if I could find one word to describe this book, I would use the word "axiom." An axiom, by dictionary definition, is "a self-evident truth." When someone uses an axiom to describe attitudes, behaviors or values, it is like turning on a light bulb. The first thing you notice about an axiom is that it is so strikingly obvious. The second thing you think is, "Wow, I wish I would have thought of that!"

There is another word found in the immense dictionaries on large wooden podiums in the old and traditional libraries. The word is "platitude". A platitude is defined in the dictionary as "a flat, dull and trite remark, especially one uttered as if it were fresh or profound." If that is what my book is about, then it is hardly an appealing description. After all, who wants to read something that is "flat, dull and trite"? A slightly more appealing definition for platitude is the one in Webster's New World Dictionary. It defines platitude as "a commonplace remark."

No matter which word you use to describe the writing that follows, I hope you find the words anything but "dull and trite." I have lived by and been taught axioms and platitudes my whole life. Instead of being "flat and dull," I have found them to be filled with meaning and folk wisdom. The people I grew up around and my Christian faith have given me important pearls of wisdom and insight. I would prefer to describe them as "truisms." These are words and phrases that help give meaning and sense to living. As I said earlier, an axiom, platitude or truism is a kind of wisdom that everyone recognizes when they hear it. It is often painfully obvious. It can be even more painful to accept and live by these axioms, platitudes or truisms.

We all have great wisdom deposited in our lives by a host of people. It's called experience. My parent's generation would call it the "school of hard knocks."

I owe a debt of gratitude to the countless individuals who have both taught and lived whatever truths there are in this book. I especially want to thank my wife of 43 years, Kathy. She has been my most important friend and inspiration. My son, Nathan and my daughter, Terra are truly my pride and joy. The older I grow, the more I understand what my own father meant on his deathbed. As I took my father's hand while he lay dying he said, "You're all I've got!" I took that to mean, "Son, remember, family is the most important thing in life."

I have served as a Christian pastor for 30-plus years. You will notice that many of the truths in this book resemble those of a Galilean carpenter's son who lived some 2,000 years ago. Forgive me if I lapse into the occasional sermon. The words of the Biblical witness are some of the most profound, meaningful, and baffling truths I have ever encountered. You can also see other books that have etched their truths and ideas on my life by reading the chapter footnotes.

In Chapter 4 I share the important value of giving 10%, saving 10% and living on 80%. As a result of these values I intend on giving 10% of all profits from <u>Just Plain Sense</u> to causes that serve to feed, clothe and care for the poor.

In the final analysis, people write and speak best about the things they truly believe in. These are the things that are just plain sense to them.

Whether you give the words from this book the name of axiom, wisdom, truism or platitude, I hope this book adds something to the satisfaction you take in living the truths that were passed down to you.

Chapter 1

Chapter 1: Summary
1. **"Never work just for money or for power. They won't save your soul or build a decent family or help you sleep at night."** [1]

The power of this simple truth focuses on work or "vocation" as an important, even God- blessed, activity of life. However, in many ways, work has become a "new religion" in our society. People spend more and more time away from other "vocations" of family and leisure. How do we find a balance?

"Never work just for money or for power. They won't save your soul or build a decent family or help you sleep at night." [2]

I had never met the lady. She passed on her wisdom as she was sitting in her wheelchair. You see the lady was going home from the hospital. We were both in the hospital elevator. I was standing and she was sitting. The wheelchair she sat in was pushed by a hospital volunteer. As the elevator was going down to the first floor, she unknowingly shared a very simple, but profound statement with the volunteer pushing her wheelchair. She was discussing how she looked forward to returning to her own home. It would be such a pleasure to be back in her own house, sleeping in her own bed. She spoke in a distinct, slow, southern drawl. Here comes the wisdom. She said, "Oh I don't have a big house but its fine for me. After all…"**you cain't but sleep in one bed at a time**."

What a wonderful attitude to carry through life! To be content with what you have and satisfied with "enough", is to be truly blessed. I am reminded of Paul's admonition to the young Timothy, "There is great gain in godliness with contentment; for we brought nothing into the world, and we cannot take anything out of the world; but if we have food and clothing, with these we shall be content."[3] Or, to quote the philosopher Epictetus, "He is the wise man who does not grieve for the things which he has not, but rejoices for those which he has."[4] Or, finally, to put it a little more cynically, "Remember, even if you win the rat race, you are still a rat!"

In his book, <u>Enough: True Measures of Money, Business, and Life</u>, John Bogle, founder and retired CEO of The Vanguard Fund writes this: "At a party given by a billionaire on Shelter Island, Kurt Vonnegut informs his pal, Joseph Heller, that their host, a hedge fund manager, had made more money in a single day than Heller had earned from his wildly popular novel <u>Catch 22</u> over its whole history. Heller responds, 'Yes, but I have something he will never have…enough.' "[5]

My first job was in the fast-paced world of sales. The products were copiers, duplicators and early fax machines.

I can remember the pressures of monthly sales quotas and competition from numerous other companies. Our office receptionist had been out sick for a period of time. Wanting to help cheer her up, I went to the local card shop and found the perfect card for her. The card read, "Please get well and come back soon…the RATS are winning." I'm sure the "rat race" feeling is one that we all can identify with on many days.

This is the book I always wanted to write. It is not because I needed the money. It is not because I hunger for fame. It is not because I need to write a confession. None of these things would do me any harm, you understand, but neither would they fill my need for written expression. Mostly I write this because I happen to believe you can live a meaningful, good and blessed life based on some of the truths that follow. The Bible and other scriptures of religious traditions are full of timeless wisdom. However, there are also many pearls of timeless wisdom passed down by the stories, sayings and lives of our loved ones, neighbors and friends. Sometimes, maybe most of the times, we are recipients of these pearls of wisdom simply by hearing them spoken. They may not always be written in books or presented in lectures by some great mind. Like the words of the lady in the hospital elevator, they are simply overheard by us and etched into our memories.

I wish I had stopped to write down that lady's name. I wish I had thanked her for her positive attitude. I would have loved to find out from whom she had received such simple and blessed wisdom. "You cain't but sleep in one bed at a time" is a piece of wisdom that I think of often as I try and understand the frenetic pace of life that surrounds so much of modern-day living.

How might your life change if you changed your attitude from one of entitlement to one of gratitude? The lady leaving the hospital exhibited gratitude for what she had, not sorrow for what she did not have. The attitude of entitlement says, "I deserve this!" or "I have a right to that!" "I can't possibly live without this or that." "I deserve my fair share." The interesting thing is that this attitude of entitlement crosses socio-economic lines. It is found in ample measure both in the rich and in the poor.

Is it just me, or do you also notice the world becoming more self-centered? Of this I am certain. We creatures have always been, to use a Latin phrase, *"incurvatus in se"*. This Latin phrase means we are turned in on ourselves rather than out to God and our neighbor. But really, we seem to relish the egocentrism of the "me first" philosophy. As Mark Twain once said, "Don't go around saying the world owes you a living. The world owes you nothing. It was here first."

T-shirt slogans and bumper stickers announce our new age of narcissism. Here are a few of my favorites: "I am the princess!" "Don't worry, you can't afford me." "As a matter of fact, it is all about me." I'm sure you could list your own favorites. Maybe you even wear one of these T-shirts. Now, I am all for having a healthy sense of humor and exhibiting a positive self-concept, but some of these shirts go beyond funny to sad.

The woman who was satisfied with her humble home was a breath of fresh air in the environment of "have more and get more." "You cain't but sleep in one bed at a time." There it was. Jesus couldn't have said it any better. Well, actually, you be the judge. What Jesus actually said is, *"Do not lay up for yourselves treasures on earth, where moth and rust consume and where thieves break in and steal, but lay up for yourselves treasure in heaven, where neither moth nor rust consumes and where thieves do not break in and steal. For where your treasure is, there will your heart be also."*[6]

Which reminds me of another true story. Chaplain Larry served as police chaplain in my town. Over the years I served as a volunteer for that police department. Chaplain Larry and I became friends. One day he told the story of a relative who lived through the difficult days of America's Great Depression. This relative had a real fear of banking institutions. He, no doubt, had seen too many friends and neighbors lose money when banks were forced to close in those dark days of the 1930's.

Larry told me that after his relative's death the family members began sorting through his personal effects. One day they got around to looking at an old car, rusting away in the back yard. It had not been driven for years. After some inspection they decided to get the keys and open the car's trunk. There, locked away from prying eyes, were bundles of cash. It was the man's personal safety deposit box. There was only one problem. The heat, humidity and years had taken their toll. When the relatives reached in to take the money out of the trunk, it literally crumbled in their hands. It had become useless!

Every time I remember Chaplain Larry's story, I can't help but think of the teacher who said, *"Do not lay up for yourselves treasures on earth, where moth and rust consume…"*

Jesus continues by saying, *"Therefore I tell you, do not be anxious about your life, what you shall eat or what you shall drink, nor about your body, what you shall put on. Is not life more than food, and the body more than clothing?"*[7]

The secret to happiness can never come from material things because we are not purely material creatures. We yearn for things that material wealth cannot give us. As much as the material is essential for survival, other things like love, security and community are also essential for our well-being. Here is the truth, "Money will buy you a cute dog, but it won't buy you the wag of its tail."[8]

You say, "Whatever do you mean by that statement?"

Well, logically speaking, why would anyone buy a dog? A dog costs money. You have to feed, groom and care for a dog. So why do we have dogs? I bet anyone who owns one can tell you instantly. We all seek things that can't be added up by a calculator. Money really does not equate to greater happiness.

"Forbes" magazine, in September 2004, had an article entitled, "It's Official, Money Can't Buy You Happiness." The article shared results of a survey comparing the Forbes 400 wealthiest persons with members of the Maasai tribe in Africa. Certainly on any objective level of material wealth, the Forbes 400 people would come out way on top when it comes to material wealth. But, as the article goes on to say, the level of happiness of these two dramatically different groups of people were virtually the same. Peter Ubel, Professor of Medicine at the University of Michigan says, "The relationship between money and happiness is pretty small." So, if you are dreaming of winning the lottery, also be prepared for some of the feelings that accompany sudden wealth. These feelings are much like the feelings of sudden loss. To be sure, instantly wealthy people feel great joy. In addition, instantly rich persons also experience fear, shame, guilt and anxiety. These feelings are much the same as the people who loose significant loved ones.

I can hear you say with Tevya from "Fiddler on the Roof", "Lord, if riches are such a curse, would you curse me a little?" But remember Professor Ubel's observation, money is not the secret to happiness. As Professor Ubel says, "The relationship between money and happiness is pretty small."

One Christmas time, many years ago, a reporter was asking President Ronald Reagan what he wanted for Christmas. President Reagan replied, *"Peace on earth."* Undeterred, the reporter continued to press for a more concrete answer.

"No, Mr. President, I mean what do you want that comes in a box?" to which, President Reagan replied, *"If you can get it in a box, I'll take it in a box."*

"Never work just for money" on the surface seems like a ludicrous statement. What in the world would you work for, if not for money? After all, you can't live on love. Or as my grandmother used to tell my sisters, "Remember, it's just as easy to marry a rich man as a poor man."

Well, let me suggest there are more important things to work for than money.

As I mentioned earlier, my first job out of college was in sales. One day, after work, I was out fishing with a sales colleague of mine. Jim stated in a categorical fashion, "Money is not a motivator." When I asked him what he meant, he said, "money is a de-motivator, that is, it will serve to discourage a worker who doesn't feel she/he is being adequately or fairly rewarded for the time and effort being put forth. But money, by itself, will not motivate on its own."

When I reflected on Jim's idea, I began to see the wisdom in his words. If money were a true motivator in life, then it would follow that the more money people made, the more they would be motivated. I don't think that is true in business, sports, entertainment or any other arena of life.

Then I began to examine what motivates me. When I began to examine what motivated me, I immediately began to think of non-material things. In my own life, pride of achievement, recognition of peers and the approval of others have been far more powerful motivators than money. I'm sure we have all met people who seem to enjoy their jobs even though they aren't at the top of society's pay scale. Conversely, we know people who, no matter how much money they make, still complain that they are overworked and underpaid. Most of the time the satisfaction, or lack thereof, is not just about money.

Work is far too important to do only for money. We spend so many hours of our life at our jobs that it important that we spend those hours for more than just a paycheck. Benjamin Hunnicutt, author of History of Work, has put it this way, *"Work has become our new religion, where we worship and give our time. As people's commitment to family, community and faith are shrinking, they begin to look to their careers to provide them with meaning, connectedness, identity and esteem."*

Here is the problem. A job was never designed to provide meaning, connectedness, identity and esteem. At the end of life, one almost never hears a worker say, "I wish I would have spent more time at the office, or the factory, or the school, or any other workplace."

What one might hear is a regret over not spending more time with loved ones. What one might hear is a regret that they didn't take the time to watch their children grow up. They may even wish that they had spent more time in giving back to their community by volunteering. Maybe they would say, in a more candid moment, "Why didn't I learn to enjoy life more?"

When my son was in his early teens he would come into my home office after school. He would ask, "Dad, would you play catch with me before supper?" I rarely turned down those opportunities. Now, as I said, I had a home office at the time. There were plenty of times I was in the middle of a project that I needed to complete. There were plenty of times I could have said, "Sorry, I just don't have the time." But, I can remember thinking to myself, *"Drop what you are doing. Take the time with him now! There will come a day when your son will stop asking you to play catch!!"* I never regretted taking the time to play catch.

Rev. Paul was a hospital chaplain and friend. He told me once, *"When confronted with the dilemma of having to be at two events at the same time…choose the unrepeatable event!"* What great wisdom. Of course, there will be times when we are faced with two unrepeatable events. Those two unrepeatable events may be happening at exactly the same time. However, I believe there are far fewer unrepeatable events than we think. Just take some time to ask the questions, *"Which one is unrepeatable? Which one is truly important?"*

"Never work just for money or for power. They won't save your soul or build a decent family or help you sleep at night." Work is important. After all, if a typical 40-hour workweek represents one-third of a typical Monday-through-Friday week, then you want to spend that time doing something you enjoy. More to the point, you want to spend that time doing what you feel "called" to do. The word vocation comes from the Latin word "vocare", to call. Work then is not just a pursuit to put bread on the table. No, work is a God given opportunity to use our time and abilities not only for our own good but also for the good of others. To find a fit between what your gifts are and a job that needs to be done can make work a pleasure instead of a burden, a blessing instead of a curse. Now, if you think this all sounds too idealistic, I want you to meet someone who treated his work as a call.

H. George Anderson was presiding Bishop of the Evangelical Lutheran Church in America from 1995 until 2001. His "call", was the highest ecclesiastical position in a 5.2 million member denomination. It, no doubt, was a job that was high stress and high satisfaction. When interviewed about his election to this office, he said, "The saying is true, he who seeks this job, deserves this job." In other words, I believe Bishop Anderson was trying to say that the office seeks the person, not the other way around. This is truly the way work ought to be.

But how would one possibly discern the right work in life with such a myriad of choices? What is the right work to do? According to Bishop Anderson, one does not find one's calling by seeking it. But, how then can a job seek us?

Maybe the secret to the question of how the right job "seeks you" begins with some serious soul-searching. What is it that you are good at? When are you happiest? When have you really felt that you made a difference? Do you have an activity that you can lose yourself in for hours? Do you prefer working with people or with things? There are countless vocational testing instruments that can help you answer these questions.

Lest you think this whole discussion about vocation is too theoretical, let me introduce you to my father. My dad immigrated to this country at the age of 18. He came to this country from his native Sweden to seek an opportunity for a better life. Ludwig Ottoson had an older brother Victor who was in the construction trades in Rockford, Illinois.

Like so many immigrants, he was forced to work in some very menial jobs just to put bread on the table. Fortunately, his older brother was there to help him get work. He mixed concrete by hand. Later, my father was able to secure a job as an apprentice bricklayer. My dad was a quick learner, good with his hands and had unbounded energy. He would work his day job laying cement blocks and bricks. He built houses, fireplaces, banks, factories, etc. He and my mom bought a 107-acre farm when I was 3 years old. I am sure he thought it was costing him a fortune in 1951, but he wanted to move his kids from the big city to the open country.

During the evenings and weekends, he would tend to the 107-acre farm I grew up on. As physically demanding as the work was, he never seemed to complain. He and my mother took pride in the fact that my dad was always in demand. He would endure occasional layoffs or recessions, but would always seem to find new work, even if it meant commuting an hour or more to a job site. He had found the solid foundation of the middle class American life.

My father used to say that he wanted his kids to be able to work with their heads instead of their hands. My father had an 8th grade education, but in the early 20th century only 6 percent of the population had graduated from high school. My dad had the foresight to know that education was the ticket to a better life. This explained his insistence on a good education for his kids. He was rewarded in this insistence by having one daughter who was a valedictorian and one daughter who was in the top 10% of her class. And then there was me, but what can I say, I probably got by on my sparkling personality.

Between the three kids, there are three bachelor degrees, two masters' degrees and a doctorate. My dad and mom knew that education was an essential step in achieving the American dream. People with an education simply had more control over their own destiny.

This, however, did not mean that my father wasn't proud of being a bricklayer. On the contrary, my mother would boast that my dad was the best bricklayer around and everyone wanted him to do work for them. That pride of accomplishment was evident every time we would drive down the streets of Rockford, Illinois. "I can remember working on that bank", he would proclaim. "That's the building we worked on during the hottest summer on record!" My dad had left his mark on places, buildings and people. The feeling of accomplishment and pride that my father exuded about his work is a sign of having a "call."

After giving birth to three children, my mother became a stay-at-home mom during my growing up years. Being a homemaker was a calling for her as well. However, my mother had another passion and call in life. She loved kids, especially kids that needed extra love. There was a period of 12 years where my mother took in 14 different foster kids. Some of these kids stayed in our home for a few months. Some stayed for years. It was work for which she received very minimal pay, but where she received deep satisfaction. That may be another sign of a calling. A calling is finding something you would be willing to do for free and then finding someone willing to pay you for doing it.

My parents would not have described their work as holy. They would probably reserve the word holy for pastors, priests and people in religious orders. The fact remains that my mom and dad were both engaged in holy work. Martin Luther, the great 16th century reformer, once said, "A milk maid can milk cows to the glory of God." Any work can be described as holy if it serves both the worker and the world. Author Frederick Buechner puts it this way, "The place God calls you to, is where your deepest gladness and the world's deepest hunger meet."

Never work just for money or power. I want to say a word about power. If you seek a position for the power that it affords you, then a motivating factor in keeping the position, is keeping the power. History is littered with people who tried to hold on to power at all costs. The consolidation and protection of power usually ends in tragic consequences for power seekers and others. Power as a motivation for work focuses on the wrong end of serving. It is about the work serving you, instead of you serving the work.

One day the followers of Jesus were jockeying for position and power. Which one of them was the greatest? He admonished them with these words, "If anyone would be first, he must be last of all and servant of all."[9] It's all about service.

At the heart of the philosophy of Martin Luther King Jr. was service. He believed that service is the soul's highest purpose. It is also the path to happiness, to greatness, and to God. He said, "You don't have to have a college degree to serve. You don't have to make your subject and your verb agree to serve. You don't have to know about Plato and Aristotle to serve. You don't have to know Einstein's theory of relativity to serve. You don't have to know the second theory of thermodynamics in physics to serve. You only need a heart full of grace. A soul generated by love."

The most honorable man I ever met was not a church leader, an executive or a famous politician. The most honorable man I ever met was Tim. Tim ran a small, one-man brake shop in Kenosha, Wisconsin. I will never forget the first time I visited Tim's shop. He had an ad in the newspaper for a free brake inspection. Since my car had lots of miles on it, I decided to get a "free" inspection. Of course, you and I both know that nothing in life is truly free, but at least I could get a professional opinion on how bad my brakes really were. After inspecting the brakes and test-driving the car, Tim said, "You don't need brake pads. Your brake pads are easily good for another 6 months." He handed me his card and told me to call him in 6 months and he would be glad to replace them.

Had I really heard it right? Was he really turning down business? I could hardly believe it, but you know what? I did take my car back in 6 months. And, I took every other car I owned to Tim for brake work. Not only that, I told everyone I knew about the man who turned down business in order to do the right thing. I told everyone I knew about a local business run with honesty and integrity. I shared the story with the local "Future Business Leaders Class" at Bradford High School. I mentioned his name in sermons. My poor wife has endured the retelling of Tim's story over and over. But, it's a story worth telling over and over, because people with character and values are what we need more of in this world.

Actually, I have been privileged to rub elbows with many great people like Tim. They have been people who are comfortable in their own skin. They don't spend a lot of time or energy being something they aren't. "Putting on airs" is the way my family might describe it. No, the great people I have met in my lifetime are the ones who go about their daily routine with integrity and honesty. As U.S. Representative J.C. Watts of Oklahoma once said, "Character is doing the right thing when nobody is looking."

The person of the week on ABC News in January 2005 was Jerry Quinn. Jerry was 52 years old and owned a bar/restaurant in Boston, Mass. He had saved up $100,000 for the down payment on a river view condo in Boston when he read an article in the New York Post about an immigrant from Ecuador who needed a kidney transplant. The mother of the Ecuadorian immigrant was willing to donate the kidney he needed. There was only one problem, he had no insurance to pay for the operation.

Jerry Quinn read about the plight of this immigrant. Being an Irish immigrant himself, he wanted to do something. He called the Post writer and said he wanted to donate to help the man.

"How much do you want to give?" asked the writer?

"The whole thing," said Gerry.

"That's $100,000. Are you serious?"

"Yeah, I'd like to do the whole thing," came back the reply.

Paying for the transplant was a gift from one immigrant to another. As Gerry met Franklin Piedra for the first time, Jerry received a hug and the words, "You are wonderful. You are an angel."

Never work just for money or for power. In a book entitled, _Let your life speak: listening for the voice of vocation_, Parker J. Palmer is deliberating on whether to take the presidency of an educational institution. It would mean more pay, status and influence. From a career standpoint it was an obvious decision. But Parker is a Quaker, and when Quakers are faced with a major decision they call together close friends to serve as a "clearness committee."[10]

Well, I'll let Parker Palmer finish the story…

"As is the custom in the Quaker community, I called on half a dozen trusted friends to help me discern my vocation by means of a "clearness committee," a process in which the group refrains from giving you advice but spends three hours asking you honest, open questions to help you discover your own inner truth. (Looking back, of course, it is clear that my real intent in convening this group was not to discern anything but to brag about being offered a job I had already decided to accept!)

For a while, the questions were easy, at least for a dreamer like me: What is your vision for this institution? What is its mission in the larger society? How would you change the curriculum? How would you handle decision making? What about dealing with conflict?

Halfway into the process, someone asked a question that sounded easier yet but turned out to be very hard: 'What would you like most about being a president?'

The simplicity of that question loosed me from my head and lowered me into my heart. I remember pondering for at least a full minute before I could respond. Then, very softly and tentatively, I started to speak: "Well, I would not like having to give up my writing and my teaching….I would not like the politics of the presidency, never knowing who your true friends are….I would not like having to glad-hand people I do not respect simply because they have money….I would not like…'

Gently, but firmly, the person who posed the question interrupted me: 'May I remind you that I asked what you would most like?'

I responded impatiently, 'Yes, yes, I'm working my way toward an answer.' Then I resumed my sullen but honest litany: 'I would not like having to give up my summer vacations….I would not like having to wear a suit and tie all the time….I would not like...'

Once again the questioner called me back to the original question. But this time I felt compelled to give the only honest answer I possessed, an answer that came from the very bottom of my barrel, an answer that appalled even me as I spoke it.

'Well,' said I, in the smallest voice I possess, 'I guess what I'd like the most is getting my picture in the paper with the word president under it.'

I was sitting with seasoned Quakers who knew that though my answer was laughable, my mortal soul was clearly at stake! They did not laugh at all but went into a long and serious

> *silence—a silence in which I could only sweat and inwardly groan.*
>
> *Finally my questioner broke the silence with a question that cracked all of us up—and cracked me open; 'Parker,' he said, 'can you think of an easier way to get your picture in the paper?'*[11]

Now, I fully understand how complicated it is to discern a true vocation or calling in life, but Parker Palmer's story is a powerful reminder of where to start.

What would you like about the job? Even as I read that question it seems foolish and impractical. A job is for earning money, right? A job is for putting bread on the table, shoes on our feet and a roof over our head, right? A job can give us greater power and prestige, right? The answer to these questions is both yes and no.

I have turned down a few jobs in my life. In the ministry we use the term "call" for the work we do. These jobs/calls are taken very seriously. They involve discernment, struggle and prayer by both the individual pastor, who is considering the call and from the congregation, which is extending the call. In some cases, the call comes not from a local church but from a regional or national office, a counseling setting, a hospital or a social service agency.

I remember well the most difficult decision I have had to make regarding a call. It was a call that, by most worldly standards, would be considered a "promotion." The work would come with a title and considerable power. This title and power was both perceived and real. I did have a close group of clergy prayer partners who helped me in my decision. (I'll speak more about the importance of having an accountability group in Chapter 6 of this book. That chapter deals with the importance of friendships).

In truth, my decision was made as I drove back from the interview. In the quiet of the drive home I thought of the quote that takes a central place on my office desk. It is a framed, hand-stitched cloth done by a dear friend, Mary Jane. The quote is at the beginning of this book and is the title for this chapter. "Never work just for money or for power. They won't save your soul or build a decent family or help you sleep at night." The quote has always served as a sort of compass for my decisions about call. I suppose some would call it a core value or a kind of true north. The two most important things that the new call were offering were money and power, the very things that could not save my soul or help me sleep at night. My decision was made.

My decision was confirmed, not by a Quaker "clearness committee", but by two people who serve very important roles in my life. My 20-year-old daughter's question was, "But Dad, would you really be happy answering that call?" My wife's response was more to the point. "Would you like this, that and the other things about this call?"

What would I like about the job? The only person I could imagine being joyful about my new call might have been my mother, who was a thousand miles away and living in a nursing home. As it turns out, she would have only enjoyed boasting about her son's new call for another 2 years. She died in 2002 and this was in 2000.

Had I taken that call I would have been committed to a calling/vocation/job that I neither was suited for or had the passion for. If I had taken the question to a Quaker clearness committee, as Parker Palmer had done, I would have come up with many reasons not to take the call.

As the Parker Palmer story so powerfully illustrates, one can take a job for entirely wrong reasons. If you take the wrong job, for the wrong reasons, both you and your employer suffer the consequences.

Does this apply to the unskilled as well as skilled jobs? What of people who have to labor at dull, repetitive or dirty work for meager wages? How do the ideas of calling and vocation apply in these circumstances? This is where it gets tricky. Martin Luther's words, "even a milkmaid can milk cows to the glory of God" seem to say that there are no "menial" jobs. Every pursuit worthy of a wage, is worthy of dignity. Any work, no matter how menial, can be done to the glory of God and the service of neighbor.

"Never work just for money or for power." I have been an ordained pastor for 35 years. I will never forget a day in 1984 when I met Susan Thompson, mission director for the Division of Service and Mission in America. She had just given an address to a church convention. Her address was about the need for pastor developers who were willing and able to plant new churches. Un-churched people need to hear the gospel message. It was a call to be a missionary, but not to a foreign land. It was a call to reach out with the gospel right here at home.

I went up to Susan Thompson after that address and introduced myself with these words, "Hi, my name is Jack Ottoson and my internship pastor once told me that I should consider being a mission developer." Susan shared this insight with me years later. "Jack, after speaking with you for 10 minutes I knew you would make a good mission developer." Why?

A true vocation seeks you, not the other way around. There are many paths that an ordained pastor can take. You can serve in small towns, big cities, old churches, new churches, traumatized churches, family churches or ethnic churches. You can enter teaching, chaplaincy work or administration. The question still remains for you and me, "What will I work for?" "How can I best match my gifts and passions in earning a living?" "What is my true call in life?" I think Frederick Buechner has it exactly right. "The place God calls you to, is the place where your deepest gladness and the world's deepest hunger meet."[12]

"Never work just for money or for power. They won't save your soul or build a decent family or help you sleep at night."

QUESTIONS FOR REFLECTION

1. What did the lady mean by, "You cain't but sleep in one bed at a time?"
2. How would you go about discerning your true calling in life so that a job seeks you and not the other way around?
3. If you were to re-prioritize your time, how would you change how you spend it?
4. Have you ever turned down a job that you knew was not "right" for you?
5. If you should never work for money or power, what should you work for?
6. If you had to come up with 3 questions to ask yourself weekly about your satisfaction with work and life, what would those 3 questions be?
7. What makes you deeply glad? What do you have the greatest urge to give? What are the world's deepest needs?

Chapter 2

Chapter 2: Summary

2. **"God doesn't count the days you go fishing"**

Starting with a story about the mayor of a town in Georgia, this chapter will explore the human need for re-creation. Woven into this chapter will also be stories of my own attempts, failures and triumphs to find "Sabbath Time" in the midst of work and family.

<u>"God doesn't count the days you go fishing"</u>

In the first chapter I shared the importance of work and call (vocation) in our lives. At first glance, work and leisure appear to be polar opposites, but I actually believe they go hand in hand. You see, the fact of the matter is, work and leisure actually complement each other. There is a rhythm in life that is broken when you have an imbalance between work and leisure. Even the most ancient of societies knew enough to break the work week by festivals or Sabbaths.

In the 1990's I served as the Protestant chaplain at Embry Riddle University in Daytona Beach, Florida. I will never forget

D. Ray. D. Ray had traveled to Daytona Beach from Georgia. His cousin, a professor at the university, had died. He came to his cousin's memorial to pay his respects. D. Ray arrived early to the memorial service, and we engaged in some small talk before the service began. This man was such a likeable person that it is easy to see how the people in his Georgia community had elected him as mayor. As our conversation progressed, D. Ray asked me a leading question,

"How old do you think I am?"

Now that is a touchy subject, but I replied as honestly as I could.

"Oh, you look to be in your late 60's," I said honestly.

D. Ray replied proudly, "I'm 85 years old!."

"Wow," I said, "I would not have even placed you in your seventies. To what do you owe your youthful look?"

His answer was both delightful and disarming. D. Ray said, "Oh, that's easy! You see, God doesn't count the days you go fishing!"

I am not sure where D. Ray had first heard that phrase. As I was to learn a few years later, it is a proverb that has been around a while. Here is the first ancient reference:

"The gods do not subtract from the allotted span of men's lives the hours spent in fishing." (Found inscribed on an Assyrian tablet-2000 B.C.)

Fishing with Ray Kaczmarek, my father-in-law, was my way of balancing work and leisure. Ray was the most positive person I have ever had the privilege of being around. To give you an example of his positive attitude I will quote from an e-mail he sent me on April 2, 2005,

"Hey, just wanted to tell you that we had a great time fishing on Friday- EVEN THOUGH we didn't catch any trophy fish. It was still a good day and Burt and I had a great time. The fishing will improve as the weather continues to improve and we'll be there to catch our limit."

Now, let me ask you, "Who wouldn't want to fish with a friend like that?" I'll describe more about balancing work and leisure in Chapter 3. For the time being we are going fishing.

Getting back to my father-in-law, I have spent lots of time out on the water with Ray. I have also been privileged to know many others who appreciate the blessings of fishing and being out in nature. Ray never seemed to care if we caught lots of fish. He just appreciated the chance to spend time on the water with his friends. Those fishing days were usually spent in good natured teasing about who was going to catch the most fish or the biggest fish. When one of the group would hook an especially good fighting fish we would ask the one who was "hooked up" if they wanted one of us to grab their pants so they wouldn't be pulled overboard.

One day I was in an especially good struggle with a nice fish. Ray leaned over to our fishing buddy, Burt, and joked, "If Jack goes overboard, make sure you grab his hat!"

Ray really liked my special fishing hat. That hat looked like it had been stolen from a French Foreign Legion soldier. I couldn't leave the dock without that special fishing hat.

Those days on the water could be filled with multiple surprises. We might witness a graceful group of dolphins breaking the surface of tranquil waters. On rare occasions we could be treated to the surfacing of a family of West Indian manatees on a quiet and steady migration to their feeding grounds. By the way, the manatee probably has the most fitting scientific name on earth. It is in the mammalian order of Sirenia.

While fishing, we were surrounded by wading and predatory birds with regal names and even more regal behaviors. Take for instance, the Osprey, a member of the hawk and eagle family. This majestic bird has a 30-40 inch wingspan and can spot a 6-inch fish from as far away as 130 feet. It has a "reversible toe" that rotates on its foot to more efficiently snatch a fish out of the water. As a matter of fact, the Osprey and Owls are the only raptors whose outer toe is reversible. This genetic uniqueness allows them to grasp their prey by locking the prey in a vice-like grip. This is particularly helpful when they grab slippery fish.[13] To watch them over the waters is to view poetry in motion.

By comparison, even the lowly pelican can give you a sense of awe. Why is that? It is because the pelican parents have to gather 120 pounds of fish for each fledgling before they leave the nest. Now that is parental commitment! Parenting doesn't come cheap for the average pelican, just like it doesn't come cheap for the average human!

Of course the biggest thrill for those who fish is the silence being broken by the whine of your fishing reel drag. The "big one of the day" is hooked and about to give you a great fight. What a blessing to experience the wonders of creation and to echo the words of Psalm 8, "O Lord, our Lord, how majestic is your name in all the earth!"

God doesn't count the days you go fishing.

Once I returned a telephone call from a clergy friend. It was on a Monday morning. Now, I have experience as a pastor, so my first question was, "Is Monday your day off?" When my colleague said yes, here was my response: "Then let me call you back on Tuesday…and for today, keep your feet up and your head down."

Everyone, no matter what their chosen line of work, needs time away from their work! There needs to be space where there are no phone calls, no urgent meetings, no computers, and no texting. Renewal requires space away from work.

In Mark's gospel it says, "And in the morning, a great while before day, he rose and went out to a lonely place, and there he prayed."[14] Jesus had just spent a whole evening among sick and demon-possessed people. The gospel writer Mark says, "The whole city was gathered together about the door."[15]

Here is another secret of good living. It is the ability to balance our work and leisure, our activity and our rest. Look at it this way. Did you ever consider how much time we waste on eating? Why can't we just "load up" with food once a day like filling up the gas tank on our car? After all, we fill the gas tank and it takes us around until we need to fill it again. Why can't we do the same by eating once a day? Ridiculous--you say? Of course, but how often do we try and do the same thing with our rest and leisure. We work long, hard hours, sometimes never taking a day off. We justify not taking time off by thinking we will make up for it on our next vacation. Then we wonder why we are so tired and out of sorts. We wonder why we get so many stress-related diseases. Here is the harsh reality: we live in a culture that neither rewards nor honors rest and Sabbath.

President Abraham Lincoln once said, "Give me six hours to chop down a tree and I will spend the first four hours sharpening the ax."

Work, without rest, is counterproductive. You will find the following story about sharpening the ax in many places and many versions, but its truth is timeless.

The story goes that in the tall trees in northern Canada, a challenge arose between two lumberjacks. Each thought he could cut more wood between sunup and sundown than the other.

It didn't seem fair, though, because one of them was the largest and strongest man in the camp. He was tough and feared by the others. The smaller man didn't seem worried, however, as they stood side by side in the forest and began to chop.

The large man was like a machine, swinging his ax, blow after blow, and rather soon his stack of wood grew larger. He never stopped. But every hour the smaller man took a break. The bigger man laughed and said, "Can't take it, aye?" The little guy just smiled.

As the sun finally lowered, sending the forest into darkness, the ringing of the axes stopped and the two tired lumberjacks compared their stacks of wood. The smaller man had a bigger stack.

"How did you chop more than me, when you took a break every hour?" asked the big man.

"Simple!" the smaller man replied, "Every time I took a break I sharpened my ax."[16]

A slightly different story, with the same truth, is a legend about St. John the evangelist. Saint John the evangelist was once playing with a partridge. Someone chided him for resting and enjoying the partridge in play rather than being busy at work.

John answered, "I see you carry a bow. Why is it that you do not have it strung and ready for use?"

He was told, "That would not do at all. If I kept it strung and ready for use, it would go lax and be good for nothing."

"Then," said John, "do not wonder what I do."[17]

Vacation comes from the Latin word for freedom and exemption. I'll never forget my first planned vacation as a newly ordained pastor. As a new pastor I had been especially diligent in my care of the "sheep." After all, I had been called to "love, serve, and pray for them…and lead them by my own example."[18] As a result, I was a little concerned about "leaving" my first flock. I loved my calling and enjoyed the variety of blessings that come with serving others. At the same time, I was also weary from that work and needed a rest. Pastor Ernst, a local retired pastor and a wonderful mentor, agreed to cover any emergencies while I was out of town. As can often be the case, a death occurred some days into my vacation. Lucy, the church secretary, recounts the telephone call as follows:

"Hello, English Lutheran Church."

"Oh, hello I am Howard's daughter. My father just passed away. May I speak with the pastor?"

"Pastor Ottoson isn't here right now. He is out of town on vacation. Pastor Ernst is helping out in his absence. Can he be of help to you?"

"Well, I really was hoping Pastor Ottoson was available. My dad is not a member of your congregation, but Pastor Jack stopped in to see my dad from time to time these last few months. I had really hoped he would do Dad's funeral. Does the pastor have a phone number where he can be reached?"

"Well," Lucy hesitated for a moment, "yes, he does, but it is a long distance call."

"Do you mind giving me his number?" the caller asked as she pressed Lucy for the number.

Lucy replied, "Well, I have an emergency number for him, but the number is in Jamaica."

"Oh, I see, he really _is_ on vacation. In that case can I have Pastor Ernst's phone number?"

Lucy responded, "Of course, I am sure he will be glad to help out!"

I am grateful that I chose to take that first vacation far away from my place of work. You see, there will always be something urgent, something pressing, something we THINK is more important than a vacation. To truly vacate your work, to truly get the rest you may need, you may not have to travel to Jamaica, but you might have to place some boundaries between you and the work you do. The message, however, is the same, no matter what your work is…occasionally you need to seek an exemption. You need, to vacate. In plain language, you need to take a vacation.

Technology has made the task of vacating our work even more difficult. The perfect example of this is a television commercial showing a man with his family on a beach vacation. The man is hiding the use of his lap top computer from his wife. He is dressing the part and even sitting on a beach chair. When his wife approaches the beach chair, he quickly hides his computer under a beach towel. Unfortunately, the man's wife sits on top of the beach towel the man has used to conceal his work computer. He has tried to hide his work obsession, but he has been busted. The look of exasperation on his wife's face tells the rest of the story. The look says, "Can't you leave your work, even for one minute, even on this beautiful beach vacation?"

We hear companies and individuals proudly using the terms 24/7. That normally means that their business and/or personnel are reachable 24 hours a day, 7 days a week. Here is the truth. No one person can be available 24 hours a day, 7 days a week. At least no ONE person can be available 24/7--indefinitely. We create the illusion of being irreplaceable, and it adds to an unrealistic vision of self-aggrandizement. After all, if lots of people depend upon me, doesn't that prove how important and valuable I am?

Now I can hear your protest already. That's easy for him to say! He had the money to take a vacation. He had someone to trust his work to while he was gone. He had a supportive (and I might add, insistent) spouse. In truth, all these objections to taking a vacation are just that, excuses. None of these excuses hold any water, unless you truly believe you are irreplaceable or are unique from all other human creatures. The fact still remains, we need rest and recuperation. Without rest and recuperation, we risk our health, our relationships and the very work we hold important.

A number of years ago, I read the obituary of a local priest. He died suddenly of a stroke at the age of 65. He had been a faithful and beloved pastor who was deeply committed to working with the poor in our community. What troubled me about the obituary was the quote by a trustee from the priest's own congregation. The trustee said, "He'd been in good health. Not one day did he miss Mass and he only took ONE VACATION in 10 years." The dramatic irony of that struck me. Here was a Roman Catholic priest, living out the classic "protestant" work ethic. The ethic that says I am valued not for who I am but I am valued for what I produce. I am valued for the sacrifices I make.

Even more ironic is the fact that this beloved priest had no doubt preached many times about his Lord's life of prayer, retreat and renewal. He no doubt had read and preached about the Sermon on the Mount, *"Consider the lilies of the field, how they grow; they neither toil nor spin; yet I tell you, even Solomon in all his glory was not arrayed like one of these."*[19]

Could it be that the commandment about Sabbath and the need for a day of rest does not apply to preachers? I doubt it. Could it be that the priest didn't have congregational and denominational leaders to encourage him to take "vacation" like the rest of his flock? Could it be that he didn't have anyone to encourage him to practice grace for himself as well as for others?

Wayne was a church leader at the first congregation I served. He was a very successful farmer, a well-respected leader in state agricultural circles and a marvelous family man. Wayne served on numerous boards and was a very busy man. He said to me one day, "Pastor, take time for rest and vacation. You can never get it all done anyway." I have remembered that and attempted to practice it. It has made all the difference.

Don't think you have the money to take a vacation? A young mother came to me early in my ministry. She complained that ever since her children were born, she and her husband had grown apart. They didn't spend as much leisure time together. They needed more time together. She defined the problem and asked me for help.

I made suggestions as to how she and her husband might carve out more private time for themselves. I asked her about activities that both she and her husband might enjoy. I suggested inexpensive places to go for a break from the kids, even if it meant going to a fast food restaurant. I even got her to think about the relatives who could give her some respite from her children.

Here is the interesting thing. She had objections to almost every suggestion I made. Either the suggestions were too costly, too impractical or they would take too much time. Finally I challenged her, "Look, you came to me asking for my help. I made some suggestions, but the ultimate decision about strengthening your marriage is yours. Change is going to cost you something. You have to decide for yourself what your priorities are going to be. It's up to you to make the changes if you want to see the results."

There is an old truism, "Your foot will never get well as long as the mule is still standing on it." I suppose the corollary to that is, "You can lead a horse to water, but you can't make it drink." If we identify a need in our life that needs attention, then the first step needs to be ours.

One of the problems with taking vacations is that we will rarely receive encouragement or re-enforcement from our workplace or our society. I can remember the first six months of my first "real" full-time job. I was a new college graduate and was working as a sales associate for a well-known copier company. I had one week of vacation coming to me in the first six months of my employment. Out of loyalty to my new employer, and a need to look good, I decided to forgo taking the weeks' vacation that was due me.

After what I considered a noble sacrifice, I didn't even get a note of appreciation. My sales manager didn't notice the noble sacrifice. None of my other colleagues noticed the noble sacrifice. The company didn't notice the noble sacrifice.

What had I sacrificed a week's vacation for? I made a commitment then and there that I would never give up any vacation days that were due to me. I have kept that commitment for the last 30+ years. I take every week of vacation that any employer offered to me. It not only was my right, it was a duty to myself, my family and even my employer.

I think the Native American culture places rest in better perspective. They have a saying that goes, "Sometimes you have to let your spirit catch up with your body." As the lumberjack story proves, a dull axe must be sharpened.

If you are the type of person who has a hard time taking time off, then I commend a book which might be of help to you. It might even make you uncomfortable enough to change!

In a book entitled, <u>Confessions of a Workaholic</u>, Wayne E. Oates coins the term "workaholic." Dr. Oates says, "Our culture has a very different attitude toward the alcoholic from the one it has toward overwork. Excessive work is lauded, praised, expected, and often demanded of a person in America... Workaholism is a much more socially approved malady than alcoholism, though both have crippling manifestations, and (workaholism) is more difficult to deal with."[20]

Life is really a balancing act between work and rest, alone time and social time, time for play and time for work.

The worst imbalance I can remember in my own life was just after our daughter Terra was born. It was a joyful time in our household as the new baby came home to join her two and a half year old brother, Nathan. While I don't remember all the details of the new baby's homecoming, you can be assured that there was the normal chaos of too little sleep and too many middle of the night baby feedings. I am sure this was mixed generously with joy, laughter and crying (mostly from the new baby).

The Sunday after the new baby arrived home was a "back to work" Sunday. I had the usual two Sunday morning worship services to lead. At that time I served a 2-point parish. I led the early service at the church nearest my home. Then I traveled my usual thirty minutes to the second church. I probably arrived back home for lunch about 1 PM. Usually, after lunch on Sundays, I looked forward to some quiet time and relaxation. This Sunday, however, was different. After lunch I put on my heavy overcoat. (It was February in northern Wisconsin.)

My wife asked, "Where are you going?"

Oh no, I had forgotten to tell her about the afternoon event I had agreed to attend! I answered like a child who has been caught with a hand in the cookie jar.

"I have been invited to speak at the 50th Anniversary of Ken & Vera," I said guiltily.

Then came the words that cut me like a knife. My wife, with tears in her eyes, simply asked,

"When is it our time?"

I made a quick apology and promised to be back as soon as possible. After another half hour drive, a routine congratulatory speech and a quick celebration meal, I finally returned home. If my "good husband" card hadn't expired, it had become seriously overdue. The words, "When is it our time?" were still ringing in my ears when I arrived back home. I doubt that there could have been an emergency big enough to call me away from home that evening. The good news is that our marriage survived. I learned from that experience. In December of 2015, my wife and I will have celebrated 43 years of marriage. Enough said.

When is it our time? Thankfully, my wife and I learned over the years to protect time with each other and time with our kids. We both worked full-time jobs. She was an educator and I was a pastor. As demanding as both of our jobs were, they also came with the benefit of flexibility. An hourly worker is not as fortunate. Kathy and I were able to use our flexibility to attend lots of our children's sports and school events.

Here is the truth. No one ever has had this saying inscribed on their tombstone, "I wish I had spent more time at the office!"[21]

God doesn't count the days you go fishing.

A few years back, when my kids were in college, I had one of the best birthdays ever. I know how hard it is for a young adult to pick out a birthday present for their parent so I decided to pick out my own present that year.

To my son I said, "You and I both love to fish. For my birthday present this year, let's go on a guided fishing trip. It would be the best present you could give me."

To my daughter I said, "There is a beautiful arboretum not far from here. For my birthday present this year, how about if you and I go to lunch at a great Thai restaurant and spend time walking through the beautiful arboretum?" I think they both enjoyed that birthday as much as I did! Oh, did I mention that I paid for my own birthday present that year? It was worth every penny. Priceless!

Garrison Keillor is one of my favorite authors and story tellers. His tales are told on the American Public Media radio program, "Prairie Home Companion." His monologues titled, "News from Lake Wobeggon", are both hilarious and touching.

My favorite "News from Lake Wobeggon" story is, "Pastor Ingqvist's Trip to Orlando", Keillor tells a story about Pastor Ingqvist and the Rural Lutheran Clergy Conference in Orlando, Florida. The essence of the story is that the church leaders at Lake Wobegon Lutheran Church vote to cut the funding to send Pastor Ingqvist to the Rural Lutheran Clergy Conference in Orlando, Florida. This is a conference that the pastor and his wife, Judi, have looked forward to attending for a long time. It was a chance for rest, renewal and "sharpening the pastor's axe."

Pastor's wife Judi is furious! Garrison Keillor recounts the tension that comes to their marriage as a result of Pastor

Ingqvist's "noble sacrifice." He gave up his vacation trip without a fight. With typical humor and sharp insight, Keillor recounts the double standard applied to "persons of the cloth." "You're only human, of course, even though you're a minister, but if you stood up in the pulpit and told them that…you were only human, their first thought would be that you had committed adultery, and their second would be with whom and for how long. So it ain't easy. And they had been looking forward to that trip!"[22] The surprise ending to the monologue will touch your heart.

Among many other themes, the story "Pastor Ingqvist's Trip to Orlando" reinforces the need for Sabbath, for rest and for renewal. It is a beautiful story. I often play it for my friends in the clergy ranks. The story allows us to laugh at our foibles, our calling and the double standards that surround the work we do.

We clergy have the unique temptation of believing the many good things people say about us. Statesman and politician, Adlai E. Stevenson said, "Flattery is alright if you don't inhale." Flattery can create a dual dependency. We can become dependent on the flattery and on the work that creates that flattery. If we are not careful, we can fall prey to the illusion that it is all about us. The fact of the matter is, no matter how gifted or talented we are, it is never all about us.

Here is one more story to convince you to go fishing, or whatever you do with your time off. It is a story taken from Major Stan of the United States Air Force. Stan had arranged for a vacation months in advance. Just prior to taking his vacation, a very important project came up at his job in the Pentagon. Major Stan went into his superior officer's office and said, "Sir, I realize an important project has just come up and I am scheduled for vacation next week. If you would like me to cancel my vacation to work on the project, I am willing to do it."

The superior officer said,

"Major, that is very commendable, but first I order you to bring me a bucket of water."

Stan thought the direct order was a little strange but carried out the order. He brought the bucket of water back to the commander. The commander said,

"Major, I want you to stick your hand into the water. Now, Major, I want you to take your hand back out of the water. Tell me, major, look closely into the water. Do you see a hole in that water?"

Stan answered, "No, Sir!"

The commander said,

"I didn't think so. Major, I suggest you take your vacation as planned."

By ordering the bucket of water the superior officer was simply saying, "The business of this department will carry on fine without you. You are not irreplaceable, so go ahead and take your vacation."

God doesn't count the days you go fishing.

I want to dedicate this chapter to my father-in-law, friend and lifelong fishing buddy, Ray. I looked forward to our weekly fishing trips. He was the most positive person I have ever met. Will Rogers, the early 20th century humorist, is quoted as saying,

"When I die, my epitaph or whatever you call those signs on gravestones, is going to read: 'I joked about every prominent man of my time, but I never met a man I didn't like.' I am so proud of that I can hardly wait to die so it can be carved. And when you come to my grave you will find me sitting there, proudly reading it."[23]

Well, if Will Rogers never met a man he didn't like, I can honestly say that I never met one person who didn't like my father-in-law, Ray. As I said earlier, he had the most positive attitude of anyone I have ever met. Whether he asked you about your work, your home town or your new car, he was genuinely interested in hearing what you had to say.

Ray's oncologist loved appointments with Ray. They would spend the first 20 minutes talking about fishing and grandkids. Then they would get around to the treatment options for his cancer.

Ray's laughter was infectious. He would often laugh so hard at his own jokes that the tears would run down his face. He loved life and he loved people.

On January 30, 2008, Ray died after a long battle with cancer. His immediate family was at his bedside. He died peacefully.

Ray provided laughter even at the end. A few minutes after he died, the refrigerator repair man called to ask if he could come the next day to fix the ice maker. I was the one to take the phone call. Despite the seriousness of the situation, the ice maker, after all, did need to be repaired. So...

From the kitchen phone came my question,

"Jean, I know it's not a good time now, but can the repairman come tomorrow to fix the refrigerator?"

Jean answered, "Yes, tell him tomorrow will be fine."

Life goes on. There are times when I want to believe Ray, safely now in heaven, orchestrated that phone call just for a little comic relief around his death bed!

Ray's desire was to be cremated. He was under the care of hospice and before the body is taken from the home, the family chooses what to dress their loved one in. For Ray, it was an easy decision. We found his favorite blue fishing shirt. But when his wife, Jean, suggested we send him dressed with his favorite fishing cap I had to protest.

"No", I said, "don't send him out with his fishing hat!" I explained my reaction by repeating the story from our fishing days...here it is again:

(Ray leaned over to our fishing buddy, Burt, and joked, "If Jack goes overboard, make sure you grab his hat!" I could hear Ray say, "If I go overboard, make sure you grab my hat!")

Work! Love! Play! Remember, God doesn't count the days you go fishing.

QUESTIONS FOR REFLECTION

1. What do you enjoy doing with your time off from work?
2. Can taking time off from work really add to your life span?
3. Who is your role model for achieving balance between work and play?
4. How does time off from work make you a better worker?
5. What excuses do you use for not taking vacations?
6. If you could create the perfect vacation... Where would you go? How long would you stay? Would you go alone, with someone else or with a group?
7. How is your balance between work and leisure?

Chapter 3

Chapter 3: Summary

"Never wrestle with a pig; you'll only get dirty and the pig will love it." Everyone has unpleasant people and situations to deal with in life. What are ways we can learn to deal with the person who is constantly negative, the one who is a persistent complainer/whiner and the situation that seems to have no good outcome available? Some chapter quotes, "The more you complain, the longer God lets you live." "Some people would complain if you hung them with a new rope."

"Never wrestle with a pig; you'll only get dirty and the pig will love it."

"Never wrestle with a pig; you'll only get dirty and the pig will love it." This old English proverb can be described as a "cliché" or a "catch phrase." The dictionary describes clichés and catch phrases as "overused," "trite" or "worn out by constant use." No matter what words you use to describe the phrase, there is no doubt about the meaning of the words.

Now, I don't know too many people who wrestle with pigs in real life. As a kid growing up on the farm, I can remember trying to corral a few pigs during vaccination time. I also remember trying to compete with my buddies to see who was strong enough to wrestle a 200-pound porker to the straw mat of the pig pen. Keep in mind, these were the days of "All Star Wrestling" and iconic names like Verne Gagne, Mad Dog Vachon and "The Crusher."

As pig pen competitors, we quickly learned how strong and determined a pig can be when a human attempts to corner it or place it on its back. Any self-respecting pig doesn't really enjoy wrestling. So what is this cliché really saying? I think it is simply this…there are some things in life that are better left undone. In other words, don't attempt the futile. You certainly can give futile attempts a try, but be prepared for very predictable results. Wrestling with pigs only gets you dirty.

Here is a much more spiritual way of putting it. "God, grant me the serenity to accept the things I cannot change, the courage to change the things I can, and the wisdom to know the difference." These words are most commonly known as the serenity prayer. It can be found in countless gift shops, it is quoted in many books and it is found on millions of plaques. It has been closely connected to the work of Alcoholics Anonymous. I bet you have never heard the rest of the prayer, attributed to theologian Reinhold Niebuhr. The prayer continues, "Living one day at a time; accepting hardship as the pathway to peace. Taking as He did, this sinful world as it is, not as I would have it. Trusting that He will make all things right if I surrender to His will, that I may be reasonably happy in this life, and supremely happy with Him forever in the next."[24]

What a simple, wise and effective prayer to guide our daily thoughts and actions! If we could only put this simple prayer to work, we could spare a lifetime of unrealistic expectations, frustrating outcomes and predictable unhappiness.

A few years ago I came across a quote that added to my understanding of the serenity prayer. Here it is. "Never underestimate your power to change yourself. Never overestimate your power to change others."[25]

In his book, <u>Depression is Contagious</u>, Dr. Michael Yapko shares these insights, "There are some wonderful people out there that can be trusted, there are some pretty unpleasant people out there who should never be trusted, and you—and everyone—must learn to tell them apart."[26] Dr. Yapko explains six criteria we can use in friendly, polite and inviting ways to evaluate whether people are trustworthy. You do not have to be experiencing depression to gain loads of insight from his book.

This reminds me of something my marriage counseling professor once shared in class. "Never spend more than one hour with a depressed person. It will not help the depressed person or you the helper."

If your first impression of this statement is like mine, you are thinking... "What an uncaring statement to make." After all, isn't listening one of the goals of helping people through their darkest days. Upon further reflection, the statement makes perfect sense. After all, the goal of counseling with individuals is not about you. It is not primarily what you can do for them, but what they can begin to do for themselves. The goal of counseling individuals is to begin helping the person in need to gain some of their own resources in the healing process. To place boundaries on the time you spend with persons in need is a reasonable thing. To set limits is not abandonment but accompaniment.

In a later part of his book, <u>Depression is Contagious</u>, Dr. Yapko says almost the same thing that my beloved marriage counseling professor said. Here is how Dr. Yapko puts it. "To preserve their own wellbeing, a responsibility each person has to him or herself, people who are not depressed sensibly pull away from those they fear may pull them down. Rather than blame them for that, the more worthy goal here is to avoid putting them in that awful position."[27] I highly recommend reading the whole book for the full context of his words of wisdom.

Some years back I went to a friend of mine for advice and counsel. At the time my friend was the director of counseling at a local social service agency. We had developed a close friendship over the years. On this visit he was serving as not only my friend but my spiritual advisor as well.

I remember sharing with my spiritual advisor the frustration I was having with my mother's use and abuse of prescription pain medications. My mother was on multiple prescriptions at the time. Those prescriptions dramatically affected her ability to function. She thought, "If I can only find the right combination of pills, I can eliminate what ails me." Years later there were many times when over medication led to 911 calls and brief hospitalizations.

Now, to be completely honest, my mother did experience severe pain, both physically and psychologically. What was most ironic about her growing dependency on prescription drugs was the fact that she had a total disdain for one of the most commonly abused drugs in our society, alcohol. My mother had personally witnessed the painful results of alcohol abuse in her family of origin, yet despite this knowledge, she could rationalize her own growing dependency on prescription drugs. Why? I believe it was due to the fact that those drugs were approved/sanctioned/prescribed by a "professional."

My father knew and witnessed my mother's growing addiction to the medications and would often threaten to get rid of the pills altogether. In addition, he would complain to me, and anyone else who would listen, that the pills were a major source of my mother's problem. At the same time, he was the one who would make all the trips to the drug store to pick up those medications. It was a textbook description of co-dependency and it was a cycle that would continue until my father's death years later.

My mother even had a brief stay in a treatment facility for chemically dependent persons. Denial and co-dependency kept her from staying and getting the help she needed to deal with her chemical dependence.

Despite years of volunteer work in two different treatment centers, I was powerless to change the situation. Even now, as I reflect on that experience, I am reminded of an old saying in treatment circles. Alcoholics and drug addicts are "Good people with a bad disease."

So, enough about the family drama. Now to the story of my spiritual advisor's advice.

My friend, spiritual mentor and counselor listened to my story as I expressed my growing frustration with my mother's vicious circle of dependency and co-dependency. Eventually he totally disarmed me with two, simple questions.

He asked, "Jack, how long have your parents been married?"

I answered, "They've been married 53 years this September."

Then came the most important question of all.

His second question was, "And what is it about their relationship that you expect to change?"

There it was. The light bulb went on. What was it, indeed, that I expected to change? As the question began to sink in, I began to accept my position of powerlessness. The irony is this. Once you begin to recognize what you do and do not have control over, you can begin to experience freedom in the midst of that powerlessness.

In the last years of my mother's life, especially after my father died, she experienced deep emotional and physical pain. I can remember sitting by her bedside as she would say, "I just want to slip away and die."

Those are excruciating words for anyone to hear, especially a son or daughter. They are words that are destined to send waves of powerlessness over us. Fortunately, in thirty years of pastoral ministry, I have tried my best never to make promises which I cannot keep.

In those times of my mother's greatest pain I would say, "Mom I can't take your pain away or promise you an easy death but I can promise you that your family will provide all the care you need until the day the Lord takes you home."

"Never wrestle with a pig. You'll only get dirty and the pig loves it." With his two disarming questions, my spiritual advisor was asking, "Do you really want to wrestle with that pig?" In other words, be realistic about your chances of success. If you truly want to wrestle with that pig, be prepared to lose or get dirty trying. My friend's questions helped me sort out the possible from the impossible, the achievable from the futile.

Sometimes, if things don't go well, you will have learned a lot. I was able to use my new understanding of "accepting the things we cannot change" in my own attempts at counseling.

I remember a man named "Bill", who came to me for help. Bill was classically co-dependent with his gambling-addicted wife. The two of them would take elaborate gambling junkets to one of the many American cities that are famous Mecca's of "lost wages." There are many such places around the U. S. A. Many tour companies are more than willing to get you there.

I asked Bill, "What do you do while your wife is in the casino gambling your life's savings away?"

Bill bragged, "Oh, I never spend time in the casino. I am out playing free golf!"

Now I was curious.

"What do you mean by free golf?" I asked.

Bill was only too happy to explain.

"Oh yes", he continued. "I get to play golf for free while my wife spends time in the casino. It's a perk from the casino."

I could NOT get Bill to see that he was just as addicted to gambling as his wife. He was part of the problem and NOT part of the solution.

As a pastor I was often asked to give counsel. In the initial meetings with people I always explained that I was not a professional and credentialed counselor. However, I have had plenty of practice in the art of listening. After a few sessions, I would often refer people to appropriate professionals. I had to place this boundary around my time with Bill. You see, I could also become a co-conspirator in his illness.

After meeting with him several times I finally told Bill that I would not see him again unless he made an appointment with a professional counselor. That professional counselor could help him work through his many issues. He never made the appointment. That sent the message to me that he really wasn't willing to take a deeper look at his behavior and illness. He was more comfortable staying the same, than he was in changing.

I wasn't surprised at his anger for my placing a boundary on our future time together. There is wisdom in this truth: "when the pain of not changing, exceeds the pain of changing… humans will change." When I forced his hand to do something concrete about his pathologies, he chose the status quo. I didn't see Bill again.

I once read that "over the fence" counseling by a friend can be as effective as paid, professional counseling. This, of course, depends on the nature of the problem. I would be willing to bet that neither a professional counselor nor a trusted friend can be of much help to a person, if that person isn't honest with him or herself. A friend (or counselor) is one who tells you what you need to know, not what you want to hear. Some have assigned this wisdom about friendship to William Shakespeare, "A friend is one who knows you as you are, understands where you have been, accepts what you have become, then gently allows you to grow." Who knows if it was Shakespeare? More about friendship will be written in Chapter 6.

Acceptance and change are not opposites. My favorite poster in college said, "Accept me as I am, so I may learn what I can become." This brings us right back to the serenity prayer. The prayer is focused on achieving the balance between accepting the unchangeable (i.e. don't wrestle with a pig) and the willingness to change the things I can change (i.e. my behaviors, my priorities, my thinking).

As was mentioned earlier, never overestimate your power to change others. In the normal course of living, we will spend a lot of time around people who love to soil others with their constant complaining and worries. I'll never forget a bumper sticker I saw years ago. It said, "The more you complain, the longer God lets you live." You can buy the bumper sticker on the internet for $3. It is a corollary to this piece of wisdom I grew up with, "Some people would complain if you hung them with a new rope." So what do we do with people like that? Our natural tendency is to try and change them (or, failing to do that, to complain to others about the fact that we can't change them). That tactic usually fails miserably.

Now, understand, I am NOT advocating isolating ourselves from family, friends and co-workers whose attitudes or behaviors cause us anxiety. No, I am in no way suggesting that approach. What I might suggest is to try and maintain a non-anxious presence around the people who constantly complain or worry. It takes practice and discipline but I believe practicing a non-anxious presence around people can be healthy for both the listener and the one being listened to.

I first learned about non-anxious presence in a book by Dr. Edwin Friedman entitled <u>Generation to Generation</u>. In his book, Dr. Friedman describes non-anxious presence this way; "Differentiation means the capacity of a family member to define his or her own life goals and values apart from surrounding togetherness pressures, to say I when others are demanding you and we. It includes the capacity to maintain a (relatively) non-anxious presence in the midst of anxious systems, to take maximum responsibility for one's own destiny and emotional being."[28]

A very common source of anxiety for people is being drawn into triangles with two other people who are in conflict. Often the attempt to triangle a third person into a conflict is a conflicted person's way of relieving the stress they feel. Hear what Friedman says about using the power of non-anxious presence. "The way to bring change to a relationship of two others (and no one said it is easy) is to try to maintain a well-defined relationship with each and to avoid the responsibility for their relationship with one another. To the extent we can maintain a non-anxious presence in a triangle, such a stance has the potential to modify the anxiety in the others. The problem is to be both non-anxious and present."[29]

The concept sounds so simple and effective, but the practice of it can be far from easy. The effects of its practice, however, are powerful.

Remember, you don't have to attend every argument or triangle to which you are invited.

The difficult part of being a listener who carries a non-anxious presence is being BOTH non-anxious and present AT THE SAME TIME. You see it's easy to be non-anxious by distancing yourself, distracting yourself or faking your interest. It's also easy to be present with a person but NOT non-anxious. We can be so present that we begin to take on the other person's anxiety, complaints and worries. This serves to only transfer the anxiety temporarily. Now instead of one anxious person there are two.

True non-anxious presence, helps bring healing by honestly acknowledging the other but maintaining separateness from the other. By being both present and separate, the concept of non-anxious presence is able to give permission for the other to share his or her feelings and story without transferring the problem over to the listener.

I didn't realize it at the time, but the best training for maintaining non-anxious presence came from playing high school football. I played defensive end on our small high school team. I can remember my high school football coach encouraging me. (actually he was screaming at me) **"Don't get sucked in!"** One of the purposes of a defensive end is to turn every play back to the middle of the field where other teammates can assist in tackling the opponent. If a fast offensive player gets to the outside of the field and you are the last defender...well, the result is usually a long gain or a touchdown. Now you know what the coach meant by screaming, "Don't get sucked in." A skilled offense will try and fake a play one direction to draw all defenders that direction. If the defensive end gets sucked in that direction and the offense reverses… well, let's just say it feels like you are standing at the train platform watching the caboose leave the station. "Don't get sucked in" is great advice for someone trying to maintain a non-anxious presence.

You might find some lines from the essay "Listening as Healing" as an excellent description of non-anxious presence.

> When I ask you to listen to me and you start giving advice, you have not done what I ask… Listen…all I ask is that you listen…Perhaps that's why prayer works, sometimes, for some people, because God is still and doesn't give advice or try to fix things. God just listens and lets you work it out yourself, staying your silent partner…So, please listen and just hear me… and we can both keep in mind that there are important times in our lives when we just need to be heard and not cured.[30]

Never underestimate your power to change yourself. Never overestimate your power to change others. Never wrestle with a pig. Accept the things you cannot change. If you aren't yet convinced of these truths, let me share another example.

There was a military chaplain who once did an informal survey of counseling issues brought to him over many years. After carefully categorizing the variety of problems that people shared with him, here's what he discovered. An amazing **92%** of the problems people brought to him were problems that those people could do nothing about (i.e. past decisions they had made, worry about things that were yet to happen, attitudes or behaviors of family members, friends or co-workers).

There is a verse in the Psalms which says, "When I am afraid, I will put my trust in you."[31] Think of the peace that would come our way if we "could accept the things we cannot change," have the "courage to change the things we can" and then have the "wisdom to know the difference between the two." We might find, as the military chaplain did, that over 90% of our problems were things over which we have no control. As a result, we could spend a lot more time focused on the 10% of our problems that we **DO** have some control over.

Whole books have been written on the topic of worry, but I want to share a few of my favorite quotes. The best one is from Mark Twain, who once said, "I have been through some terrible things in my life, some of which actually happened." Another favorite saying is a Swedish proverb that goes, "Worry gives small things big shadows." How about this one by William Ralph Inge, "Worry is interest paid on trouble before it is due."

There is a video program entitled "Make It Simple." It is a resource produced by The Evangelical Lutheran Church in

America. In this video, Barb Debski, states that her mom used to call worry, "the night time what-if monster."[32] What a powerful metaphor for the concept of worry. "The night time what-if monster" lurks under and around our bed trying to keep us from peaceful sleep. As is true of most monsters under and around our beds, the monster is 100% imagination and 0% reality. What if we could find tools to confront this monster and tame it?

What if we tried living out Reinhold Niebuhr's serenity prayer for a week, a month or even a year?

Try this. Make a simple chart and call it your "complaint/ worry inventory"--(any appropriate name will do). As you catch yourself complaining or worrying, don't fight those ideas, just jot those complaints or worries down. Don't judge your complaints and worries as being good or bad. Those complaints and worries belong to you, so take charge of them by putting them on paper. After an hour, a day, a week, a month or a year, place a check mark in the "can be changed" or "cannot be changed" column. Now, take a look at the results for yourself. How many complaints or worries are under the "can be changed" column? If more than **50%** are things that can be changed, I suggest you get to work on them. However, if you are like most of us, the vast majority of your complaints or worries are in the "cannot be changed" category. The mere fact of knowing this is a powerful starting place in bringing you increased peace. Give it a try. What do you have to lose except your worries or complaints?

Jack A. Ottoson, M.Div.

MY COMPLAINT/WORRY INVENTORY	CAN BE CHANGED	CANNOT BE CHANGED
1.		
2.		
3.		

To "accept the things I cannot change", should not be used to give up on change or to avoid legitimate challenges. So, we sort out those things that we have a legitimate chance of changing from those that--pardon the phase--don't stand a prayer.

It is said, "You never learn anything the second time you are kicked by a mule." I learned the meaning of that expression the hard way growing up on the farm. I didn't learn it by literally getting kicked by a mule, but by pulling a manure spreader.

Let me explain.

Ever since I was young I learned the value of frugality and efficiency. For instance, when plowing a field you begin at the center of the field and work your way to the edges. The reason is simple…by starting in the middle, you have very little wasted motion. Your plow is in the ground almost 100% of the time, and, if you have planned it out correctly, you have no "wasted passes" where you are driving the tractor, burning up gasoline and not turning up any soil.

This philosophy does not work as well if you are driving a manure spreader. As the weather warms in the springtime, winds can be powerful. I think you know where I am going here, but bear with me.

The first time I helped with spreading manure at the family farm I got the job of pulling the manure spreader with our trusty tractor. Using another special tractor, equipped with a frontend loader, my father would load up the manure into the spreader. It was my job to drive the spreader up and down the field as this amazing piece of equipment sprayed manure out the back end.

The manure spreader is an amazingly efficient machine. It has a conveyor belt built into the bottom of its metal frame. This conveyor steadily moves the manure to the back of the wagon box. When the manure reaches the end of the box, a series of rotor-like blades, (picture here a giant roto tiller) catches the manure and flings it out the back.

Being frugal and efficient, I realized that I could time my trips from and back to the cattle yard so that my manure spreader would be working the whole time and completely empty by the time I returned for a "fresh" load. This involved spreading the load driving both south and north. This is all fine and good except for the first time I drove out of the feedlot into a stiff breeze. You guessed it, everything went just great heading into a stiff head wind but when I went to turn toward the barn, the wind was at my back and I still had half a load to spread… well, you can figure out the rest of the story. Suffice it to say, I learned the meaning of the words, "never spit into the wind" in a very graphic way. Wasted fuel or not, when there was a stiff wind, I learned to spread manure in only one direction--into the wind.

So, change the things you can and adjust your sails to changing winds if you must.

In a 1968 San Francisco speech, (Leroy) Eldridge Cleaver used a phrase that would define the attitude of an entire generation of young adults. In that speech Cleaver said, "You are either part of the solution or part of the problem." It was a call to "change the things we can." Refuse to play the victim. Make a difference!

As important as "accepting the things we cannot change" is to our serenity, we dare not forget the second part of Reinhold Niebuhr's prayer. "The courage to change the things I can", helps us focus on our legitimate power. We can be change agents in this world. One of my favorite prayers is short, simple and powerful. "I am only one, but still I am one. I cannot do everything, but still I can do something; and because I cannot do everything, I will not refuse to do the something that I can do."[33]

"The courage to change the things I can", focuses on our ability to change things. Are there goals to be accomplished? Are there human rights to be claimed? Are there wrongs that can and must be remedied? Is there forgiveness to be asked for and amends to be made?

From 1998 until 2007, I served a brand new congregation, Hope Lutheran Church in Daytona Beach, Florida. The church was in the process of paying down its land debt, seeking construction bids for a new building and applying for permits to construct a new building. After the celebration and dedication of the new church building in 2007, I decided to create a journal of the trials we went through along the way. I titled it "Hurdles & Roadblocks." What an eye opener!

What was the final number of hurdles and roadblocks? I came up with no less than 70. There is a saying that goes, "Know that if God sends you down rocky paths, God will also provide you with strong shoes."

I often look back on those trying times with gratitude. Mostly, I am grateful that I never knew which roadblock was coming next. Some of the roadblocks were big and some were small, but all of them were frustrating. In those 9 years, we dealt with no less than 30 professionals and agencies. We had delays caused by bureaucracies, hurricanes, construction material shortages, price hikes and lack of money.

Toward the end of those long and challenging years, I was walking through a local store and was captivated by a poster. It was an aerial view of an extremely difficult golf hole. The green of this particular golf hole was perched on the edge of a ragged and rocky coastline. The caption below the picture said, *CHALLENGE: The harder the course, the more rewarding the triumph*. In one short sentence, the poster captured the long years of frustrations and hopes. I bought it and immediately hung it in my office. I think it helped me over the last 15 hurdles in the construction process.

Some things are worth the struggles. Some things can be changed. Looking back on those years of trials, I often say that the three "P's" got me through. Those three "P's" were patience, persistence and prayer. I also used to joke with anyone who would listen that any professional, agency or bureaucracy who thought they could deny our church the legitimate right to build a new building on the property we had paid for--had never watched me play racquetball. I have a fierce competitive streak in me.

Some things are worth fighting for. The reason they are worth the struggle is because you believe in the goodness of your actions and the right of your cause. God grant me the courage to change the things I can.

I believe public opinion and public policy have changed regarding the church. Receiving zoning and permits for churches is much more difficult in today's society. If I had to guess, I would say that many would hold the position that granting a church the right to build a building takes a valuable and taxable piece of land off of the tax rolls. After all, there are already plenty of churches out there.

My opinion is this. The "social value" provided by a new church is as important as the social value of many other non-taxable institutions like fire stations, police stations and public libraries. So, yes, some things are worth being exempt from the tax rolls.

To conclude my chapter, I want to say that there are two phrases in the English language that often give us the most trouble. They are "if only" and "when I."

"If only" is the first trouble maker. "If only" I had done this. "If only" I hadn't done that. "If only" I had more of this. "If only" I had less of that. To live with the "if only" is to be trapped by our past and to let that past define our future.

My father used to say, "I have no regrets." I always thought that was an amazing thing to say. How could anyone be so confident, (or so arrogant), to say that?

But notice, he didn't say, "I haven't made mistakes." He merely said, "I have no regrets." It is not that he had never made mistakes. It is not like he didn't know that he could have done some things better. He just said, "I have no regrets." In other words, I am not going to allow my past to define my present and future. I have done the best I could and am willing to accept that and move on.

"We are products of our past but we don't have to be prisoners of it."[34] This is how Pastor Rick Warren describes human potential. To be trapped by the words "if only" can give the impression that we are victims of our past. There is a big difference between being products of our past and being victims of our past. To be a victim of our past, presumes that we are a casualty of what has gone before us. To be a product of our past, presumes we are a work in progress. For my money, I would rather be a work in progress, wouldn't you?

You might consider the wise counsel of a dear friend and colleague of mine. Sister Francine was a professional educator and a school principal. Sr. Francine moved to Kenosha, Wisconsin to take the call to be the chaplain of the county jail. I was serving on the local jail chaplaincy board at the time and had the privilege of working with Sr. Francine. She had the rare mix of qualities needed for jail chaplaincy: toughness and compassion. With a grin on her face, she would often tell people that God prepared her well to work with convicted criminals by calling her first to be a junior high school principal. As Sr. Francine put it, "There are no better con artists in the world than junior- high boys."

I will never forget our discussions about our work with men and women at the jail. Sr. Francine would often talk about listening patiently to the difficult and tragic stories of the inmates. However, after patient listening and an understanding heart, she would often get around to this question: "John/Mary how long do you want to keep singing that tune. When do you want to learn to sing a new tune?" It was Sister's way of announcing the good news that they did not have to live by the old tunes.

They could and must learn new tunes if they were serious about turning their lives around. You see, listening to Sr. Francine was about preparing for change, or as one therapist has said, "Accept me as I am, so I may learn who I may become." Change really begins as we learn to accept ourselves "warts and all" and believe that change is possible.

"When I" is the second phrase in life that often gives us trouble. "When I" presumes that life will somehow be more complete "when I" get that big promotion, "when I" finally move to my dream home in that dream location, "when I" graduate, "when I" do this or have that. Many years ago I found the essay entitled "The Station" by Robert J. Hastings. It illustrates the twin thieves of regrets and fear, embodied in the power of "if only" and "when I." Here are a few lines from the essay.

"The Station" written by Robert J. Hastings

Tucked away in our subconscious is an idyllic vision. We see ourselves on a long trip that spans the continent...

Once we get there (ie: the final destination) so many wonderful dreams will come true and the pieces of our lives will fit together...

Sooner or later we must realize there is no station, no place to arrive at once and for all...

Regret and fear are twin thieves who rob us of today...

Life must be lived as we go along. The station will come soon enough."[35]

And, "Never wrestle with a pig, you'll only get dirty and the pig will love it."

QUESTIONS FOR REFLECTION

1. When was the last time you were engaged in a contest you could not win?
2. If you were to list your most common complaints, what would the top three be?
3. Is there anything about these top three complaints that you have power to change?
4. How might following the "serenity prayer" give you increased peace?
5. Have you ever felt trapped by a situation you could not change? What did you do? Who did you go to for help?
6. Who was the last person you tried to change? How did that work for you?
7. What is a situation you have been in where practicing non-anxious presence would have truly helped?
8. Have you ever been triangled into a conflict between two people? How did it turn out?
9. Did you try listing your complaints/worries? What did you learn?
10. What roadblocks and hurdles do you face to a more fulfilling life?

Chapter 4

Chapter 4: Summary

"100 years from now it will not matter what my bank account was, the sort of house I lived in, or the kind of car I drove, but the world may be different because I was important in the life of a child."[36]

To truly make a difference in life one must sort out the trivial from the essential, the routine from the urgent. Using examples from every day ministry experiences I hope to illustrate the importance of setting and living by priorities in everyday life. Living by priorities may actually help us to see that there are far fewer emergencies in life than we think.

"100 years from now it will not matter what my bank account was, the sort of house I lived in, or the kind of car I drove, but the world may be different because I was important in the life of a child."[37]

I was talking with my long-time friend, Tom, one day. I asked him to finish this sentence, "If you don't stand for something…" Tom immediately replied, "You will fall for anything."[38]

My friend could not recall the first person or place he had hear that phrase, but I could. "If you don't stand for something..." came up in the context of an adult Bible Study. The adult study was held in the church kitchen at the small, rural church Kathy and I attended. That church was in Tom's home town. It was Tom's home church.

I heard "If you don't stand for something..." quoted by a prominent citizen of that small, rural town. My wife and I had moved there after I graduated from college. I had been called to my first "real" job, and we rented our first home in that small, rural town.

As I said above, this was Tom's home town. Where had he heard this wisdom? How had it been so imbedded in his memory that he could recall it in a flash? I believe the axiom, "Stand for something..." was part of the fabric of that community. This was a community, like many other communities, where your word means something. It is a community where promises didn't take a five page contract to enforce. Coincidentally, it was very similar to the town I was brought up in.

It was not the prominent citizen's social or economic status that impressed me. What impressed me was his plain sense approach to life. Forty two years later, "Stand for something, or you will fall for anything", is one thing I remember about that adult Bible class. The truth of that phrase was passed on in a tiny church kitchen, filled with folding metal chairs and giant ideas.

One year prior to hearing "If you don't stand for something, you will fall for anything", I was sitting around an interview table with four or five sales managers from a major copier company. It was the last round of interviews for sales positions opening up in that company. A question was posed by Carl, one of the interviewing managers. The question was simple enough.

"Jack, where do you see yourself in four or five years?"

Now, it doesn't take a brilliant mind to see the motivation behind that question. I had seen the types of cars parked in the lot outside. I had also noticed the upscale décor in their district sales office. It was clear that material success was a high priority in this company. So, my answer was:

"I would like to enjoy enough financial success in my career to eventually buy my own home and have a nice car. In addition, I would like to improve my knowledge and skills in this company so I can advance myself."

That was a pretty safe answer but my conscience wouldn't let me stop there, so I continued.

"While I am as interested as anyone in improving my financial and work position, I also have a belief that my success should be shared with others around me. I hope that someday the success I achieve will help others who are less fortunate than me."

In a cynical and sarcastic tone, Carl asked me this follow up question: "Well, if that is the case, then why don't you go into social work?"

What would I do now? I clearly had not scored any points by bringing up my ideas about sharing my success with others.

I responded, "Well, actually the work of sales really does have an element of social work to it. It is about providing business tools so that customers can be successful. It is about working with people to solve their problems with the products your company provides."

I can remember leaving that interview with the distinct impression that I had blown it.

But, I hadn't blown it. One of the other interviewers in the room that day would eventually hire me. Harry, the manager who hired me, was looking for a sales associate who could be trusted to manage an outlying territory. A previous salesman had proven to be unreliable and unethical in some of his dealings. To put it bluntly, Harry needed someone he could trust. He needed someone who was not just looking out for number one or looking to make a quick buck. He needed someone who would also look out for the long term interests of both the customer and the company.

To this day, I believe I got the job with that company because I expressed a value system that was <u>both</u> about receiving and giving back. I was standing for the belief that life is about giving something back. Only later did I discover that at one time in his life, Harry, my new boss, had considered a religious vocation. He had chosen a business career instead, but that did not mean that he left his religious principles behind. It pays to "stand for something."

Today's way of phrasing it might be, "finding and keeping your core values." Identify what you believe from the core of your being. Practice that core belief in your family, your work and your leisure. Set your priorities in life and stick to them.

Aren't sure of what your values and priorities are? A good place to start is by doing an inventory of how you spend the bulk of your time and your money. This is usually an important indicator of your central values and priorities.

What you believe in, matters. Who you follow, matters. It is not just about you. Your stance in life affects the lives of others. Stand for something, or you will fall for anything.

When Forest Witcraft said, "but the world may be different because I was important in the life of a child," I believe he was lifting up the essentials to a truly satisfying life.

Another wise teacher, William James, said, "The great use of life is to spend it for something that will outlast it."[39] Witcraft and James knew that there were enduring values and priorities that outlast the lives we have on this earth. The secret to life then, is to sort out the transitory from the enduring, the temporary from the eternal.

Enduring and eternal values have been espoused by prophets, sages and holy persons through the ages. In his book, <u>Giving to God,</u> Mark Allan Powell recounts how radically lives were changed as they came into contact with a man called Jesus of Nazareth. "Disciples leave their boats...Levi leaves his tax office...blind Bartimaeus leaves his coat...a rich man sells his possessions...The basic point seems to be that we have a *need* to give. Stewardship, then, is not just about our meeting the needs of the poor, or the needs of our church, or the needs of any particular charity—it is about fulfilling our own need to give as well."[40]

So, with all due respect to Carl, who cynically said, "then why don't you go into social work", here is what I would say. We can't help but be engaged in social work. Our work, our family, our recreation and our lives are all about social work. We are called to be both givers and receivers. Giving is built into our very nature. To deny our need to share our time, our talents and our wealth is to deny a basic part of who we are as human beings. I will say more about our time, talents and wealth later in this chapter.

Chapter 2 of this book is titled, "God doesn't count the days you go fishing." That chapter was about balancing work, leisure and family. In that chapter I shared a time when I was out of balance between my work and personal life. How did I know I was out of balance? For one thing, I had a loving wife to remind me. I also knew I was out of balance by remembering the core values and priorities I had set for myself upon graduation from theological seminary. Let me explain.

In the last year of seminary, all seniors are required to submit a senior thesis. It is a paper that basically describes what you believe and why you believe it. To have a little fun, and to provide more entertainment value for the senior seminar committee, I did my paper on <u>The Parables of Peanuts</u>[41] by Robert Short. Short's book takes cartoons from the Charles Schultz comic strip and delves into the deep theological significance of those cartoons.

Charles Schultz was a deeply religious man and faith shows up front and center in many of his cartoons. In addition to being a great cartoonist and humorist, he was also an astute theologian. <u>The Parables of Peanuts</u> is both an interesting and funny read.

The senior thesis committee was impressed enough with my senior paper to give me a passing grade and to recommend me for graduation and ordination into pastoral ministry.

The senior interview committee had four professors. They all had very serious looks on their faces. As the interview was coming to an end, it looked like a passing grade was fairly assured. Then, I was asked if I had anything else to add. I hesitated a minute. Just like the sales interview years before, I couldn't leave well enough alone. I did have one more thing to add. Here is what I said,

"I want to express my gratitude to the faculty for preparing me to serve as a pastor. However, as much as I deeply desire to serve as a pastor in this church, I need to share two things that I am not willing to sacrifice for this work. I feel the need to share these two things both for my own benefit, as well as for the benefit of the churches I will serve. Simply put, I will not sacrifice my personal health or my family for the work I am about to embark upon."

There was a silence in the room. I am not sure many seniors had ever quite put it so bluntly, but there it was. I laid it out in the most honest way I knew how. They could accept or reject those two values and priorities, but I needed to set them out from the very beginning.

There was a kind of silent assent in the room. The nods by the gray-haired men in the room basically said, "We agree with you."

You see, I believe every one of the mentors in that room knew the importance of core values and priorities. Probably every one of them had broken a few of their own core values and priorities in their combined years of ministry and teaching.

Knowing what those core values and priorities are, helps you to stay true to your own self. None of us is ever able to maintain those values and priorities one hundred percent of the time. The point is, when we have thought about those values and priorities ahead of time, we have created a reference point for ourselves.

As any land surveyor knows, to do a proper survey you have to locate a "point of beginning." With that reference point you will know how to proceed or how far you have wandered. You will also know what direction leads you back to the "point of beginning."

As Alice in Wonderland says, "If you don't know where you are going, any path will do."[42]

Now, I fully realize that we all have to balance multiple callings in life. We have calls to be sons, daughters, wives, husbands, parents, employers or employees.

Here is the claim I was staking out at the beginning of my pastoral calling. The claim is this. Family and health are at the same priority level as the calling to do "pastoral work." As I said, it was as much for my own benefit as it was for the churches I would eventually serve. Setting core values to follow in the very beginning of my pastoral work was, as I said, similar to the work of a surveyor staking out a "point of beginning."

Years later, I would be reminded of those core values at a special gathering of clergy. We were called together by our local church leaders. The occasion was a seminar about professional ethics and sexual boundaries as it relates to the clergy profession.

Now, at first blush, it is obvious to most observers that a transgression involving finances or sexual boundaries by a pastor is wrong. The public disclosures of wrongdoing by clergy (and other public figures) make the news headlines all too frequently. As humans, we often take interest and delight in the fall of public figures. Today is no different than previous generations in this regard.

There is an interesting irony about these "voluntary" professional ethics seminars. The irony was revealed to us by church leaders. The colleagues who <u>need</u> to hear the information the most, are the ones who are "too busy" or consider themselves "too important" to attend. On the other hand, those who are at the least risk for professional ethics violations are the ones who most faithfully show up. Coincidence? I think not. So, these seminars were kind of like "preaching to the choir."

Here's a sad story that was shared by one of our respected church leaders. He described a situation where the pastor had crossed a sexual boundary with a person he counseled. Simply put, the pastor had an affair with a woman in his congregation. The effects of this behavior is devastating for the persons involved in the affair, the spouses, the congregation, those called to leadership in the church at large. You get the picture.

What was most revealing was a single quote from the wife of the pastor who had crossed the sexual boundary. Her words come as both a surprise and a warning.

She said, "My husband committed adultery with the church, long before he committed adultery with the other woman."

Setting values and priorities may not grant immunity from transgression, but, to use the church leader's words from this chapter's beginning, "If you don't stand for something, you'll fall for anything."

"He committed adultery with the church, long before he committed adultery with the woman." Those quoted words have had a profound effect on me for over thirty years. They illustrate better than anything else the point I am trying to make. You have to know what's most important to you, and then try to live out those values and priorities.

J.C. Watts was a U.S. congressman from Oklahoma. He put it this way, "Character is doing the right thing when no one is looking."

Here is another way of putting it. Dr. Dudley Riggle, former chaplain of Carthage College in Kenosha, Wisconsin, describes the essence of true ethics or character this way.

How you would conduct yourself if:

a. You knew you could get away with it.
b. No one would ever know.

Years ago I had a clergy colleague express surprise that I made a yearly commitment to take vacation during the second week of December. December 16th is my wedding anniversary. What was most surprising to my colleague was the fact that I would take vacation time in the middle of a church season called Advent.

You see, Advent, coming right before Christmas, is usually packed with lots of extra activities and special gatherings. In my own defense, before I left to celebrate our anniversary, I often prepared Christmas services ahead of time and I came back in plenty of time to participate in the annual Sunday School Christmas Program.

Here's the truth. I was a husband long before I became a pastor. My wife and I were married some eight years before I was ordained. Therefore, I was called to be a good husband before I was called to be a good pastor. Of course, I'm not saying you can't be both, but let me continue.

The anniversary of my marriage is a higher priority in my mind than a particular week or season of the church year. Frankly, the second Sunday of Advent pales in significance when compared to my wedding anniversary. I had a pointed and direct answer to the colleague who could not understand taking a December vacation. Here's what I told him.

"To me it's pretty simple, if the anniversary of your marriage is more important than the second Sunday of Advent then you won't have a problem taking your vacation the second Sunday of Advent."

In thirty years of pastoral ministry I never had anyone question my decision to take vacation on the second Sunday of Advent. Of course it wouldn't have really mattered if they had. I would have taken it anyway.

Years ago I was captivated by a particular quote about marriage. I had written down the quote, but I didn't know who said the words. That mystery has been solved thanks to a search on the internet. The quote centers on the issue of marriage and priorities. First, let me introduce the man whom I am quoting.

In the 1950s, John Paul Getty officially became the first billionaire on the face of planet earth. Mr. Getty had made his first million in 1916 at the age of 24. He was one of the most famous industrialists of the early twentieth century and the founder of Getty Oil Company. He is a fascinating man to read about. If ever there was a life that proved the adage "money can't buy happiness", it was the life of John Paul Getty.

Here are John Paul Getty's own words on marriage, "I hate to be a failure. I hate and regret the failure of my marriages. I would gladly give all my millions for just one lasting marital success." He also said, "A lasting relationship with a woman is only possible if you are a business failure."[43]

Those two quotes fascinated me. Is it any wonder that John Paul Getty was married five times? Now, I am no expert on Mr. Getty, nor do I presume to judge the circumstances around his five divorces. It just seems to me that those two quotes presume that he understood marriage as a business transaction and not a relationship. In a business transaction, you win or lose. In a relationship, you give and take. Maybe, you are even called on to compromise a little?

So, the question regarding priorities and marriage becomes, "Can I have both a successful work life and a successful marriage?" The qualified answer is yes, but not unless you are willing to balance your life between the two.

I really like this statement, "I came from a very wealthy family; we just never had much money." Have you ever considered the wealth, both material and non-material, that has been passed down to you? It is as much a part of your heritage as the color of your eyes or your height.

Gatorade Beverage Company released a commercial on October 23, 2006. The theme of the Gatorade add was, "I want to be like Mike." It was centered on Michael Jordan, arguably the most famous basketball player in the 20th century. The ad, televised around the world, was so popular that it was seen by billions of people. The musical tune was recognized by a whole generation. It was written to sell Gatorade products.

Michael Jordan was the most recognizable athletic icon of his day. You can still search for and find that famous ad on the internet. Basically, the message was this; I want to be like Michael Jordan. I want to be as talented, as rich and as famous as Mike.

With all due respect to Michael Jordan, I would rather be like my father-in-law, Ray Kaczmarek. I think once you read a portion of his eulogy, you will understand why this is true. Here are some thoughts about Ray from the eulogy, given by Pastor Tom Sublett of Ormond Beach, Florida.

Ray was one of the most lovable persons I have ever known. Dr. Chris Alexander, Ray's oncologist, once said this to his daughter Kathy, "Your dad is one of my favorite patients."

Does that surprise any of you? Ray is one of those rare people everyone seemed to like. Maybe it was because of his "attitude of gratitude." Ray loved people and they loved him in return. In his eulogy, Jack Ottoson wrote: "Ray rarely wasted time being critical of people...which is probably the reason that you would be hard pressed to find many people who didn't like Ray. You would also have a hard time listing people that Ray didn't like. He always looked for the best in people and treated everyone with the utmost respect." It was easy to love Ray.

Ray was also one of the most loving persons I have known. His life reflected the words of the Apostle Paul, "Therefore, be imitators of God, as beloved children. And walk in love as Christ loved us and gave himself up for us, a fragrant offering and sacrifice to God" (Eph. 5:1).

Jack remarked: "Ray is probably the only person I know who could go in for a CT scan, or a lung biopsy, or a chemotherapy treatment and come back talking about how kind the nurses were, or how the room was so clean, or that his doctor spent a little time talking about fishing." Those care takers who have to deal with traumatized people day in and day out loved Ray. They knew he loved and appreciated them, even under such circumstances.

In his eulogy, Jack expresses the family's gratitude for Ray's love. "For the 'attitude of gratitude' you spread to every person you met. For the kindness and devoted love you showed to Jean, your wife of 56 years. For the way your eyes lit up and filled with tears when you spoke about your daughter Kathy and your son Keith. Thank you for accepting into your loving family your son-in-law Jack and daughter-in-law Teresa. For the wonder and pride in your voice when you talked about your grandchildren Nathan, Terra, Drew, Chase and Reed. Thank you! Your 'attitude of gratitude' will be a constant reminder for us to remember what we have in life, rather than what we want."[44]

"100 years from now it will not matter what my bank account was, the sort of house I lived in, or the kind of car I drove, but the world may be different because I was important in the life of a child."

Ray was a very wealthy man. He exuded that wealth by being grateful about everything in his life. He was raised by Polish immigrant parents. His father drove a bread truck for a living. Despite these humble beginnings, or maybe because of them, he learned early on to be grateful for all things.

It will come as no surprise to you that the family of Ray Kaczmarek received an amazing amount of heartfelt condolences upon his death. The world is a different place because Ray genuinely cared about people. He touched countless people with his rarefied attitude of gratitude. Ray's occupation was work as a salesman, but he was really a social worker at heart.

Priorities help us focus on the essentials in life versus the trivial. As the chapter title says, there are very few material things that will last for one hundred years or more. Most bank accounts will be long gone, many houses will no longer be standing, and most cars will be either consigned to the scrap heap or recycled.

Acts of kindness are a different thing. Acts of caring and timeless words of wisdom are passed on generation after generation.

Ask any person who has overcome childhood adversity and poverty. They will usually describe an adult who was their role model or savior. That adult may have been a parent, grandparent, sibling, aunt, uncle, coach, teacher or any combination of the above. Come to think of it, a child doesn't even have to come from adversity to have an adult hero or heroine.

Ask anyone you know to finish this statement.

I have become the person I am today largely due to the influence of _____.

In most cases, it will only take that individual a few seconds to think of special people who have dramatically shaped their lives. It is said, "a teacher affects eternity, they can never tell where their influence stops."[45] The world **IS** different because countless people made a difference in your life as a child.

Often grandparents have served as the most influential adults in the lives of children. I have often wondered why this is so. In many cases it is the mere fact that they are the ones with the greatest abundance of time, patience, care and love. They are usually experts at passing on that time, patience, care and love. They are old enough to appreciate the need of every person to be special.

I was blessed to have a set of exceptional grandparents on my mother's side. They loved me and enjoyed having me around. My paternal grandparents had died in Sweden many years before I was born.

My favorite place to spend summer vacations was at my grandparent's trailer on the lake. By all vacation resort standards, their trailer was a primitive place with few of the comforts of home. To paraphrase the quote earlier in this chapter, "My grandparents were very wealthy people, they just never had much money." Their trailer however, was filled with love and learning. I am deeply indebted to my grandparents.

Any patience and fishing skills I have, I owe to my grandma and grandpa, Ruth and Gust Gustafson.

I could go on to describe what those simple vacations taught me, but there is one point that is abundantly clear. The most valuable thing my grandparents gave me was their time! It is the most precious gift an adult can offer. The saying is true, "the best inheritance a parent can give their children is some of their time today."[46] I would bet if I gave you a few moments, you could name a few of the saviors, heroes and heroines in your own life. If they are still alive, thank them today. Tomorrow, may be too late.

A few years ago I had the privilege of attending the high school commencement of my nephew, Drew. The main speaker was Supreme Court Justice, Clarence Thomas. Justice Thomas addressed the graduating class of Quince Orchard High School of Gaithersburg, Maryland. He emphasized the importance of the three F's. Those F's are faith, family and friends. It was a speech filled with grace. Justice Thomas said, "Faith, family and friends will be there even when we don't deserve them."

In his remarks, Justice Thomas reminded the students to thank the people who were important role models in their lives. He shared a story about his 8th grade teacher. She had just celebrated her 90th birthday. Justice Thomas still visits the nun, who is now retired from teaching. On one of his latest visits, the good sister was telling him how she was in the process of arranging for all her personal effects to be given away upon her death. As she spoke of this, she looked at a photo on her dresser. It was a photo taken of her and Justice Thomas at a special event. She said to Justice Thomas, "And this picture, this goes with me in my coffin." The world may be different because I was important in the life of a child.

My wife and I aren't big picture takers. We can go on a two week vacation and take less than a dozen pictures. This should be a real relief to my kids who will eventually have to sort through those old, worthless, photographs when my wife and I are dead and gone.

Sometimes I wonder what my kids will argue about when my wife and I enter our eternal reward. I hope their arguments are about sentimental items, rather than about money.

If they choose to fight over sentimental items, I can think of three items that might be worth fighting over.

The first item is a photo collage. At the center of the collage is our family photograph. Surrounding this family photograph are the photos of my children's grandparents and great grandparents. That photo collage represents over one hundred and forty years of family history. Amazingly enough, the collage also represents three hundred plus years of married life. Most of the great grandparents and grandparents in that photo collage were married 50 years or longer.

The second item worth fighting over is a photo collage depicting the various vacations we have taken with our kids. In that collage are pictures from Florida, Arizona, Sweden,

Jamaica and many other places. Far more important than the places, are the memories and stories associated with those places.

There is yet a third photo collage. This collage has photos taken during my kids growing up years. On that photo collage is the quote from this chapter, "100 years from now it will not matter what my bank account was, the sort of house I lived in, or the kind of car I drove, but the world may be different because I was important in the life of a child."

I hope before the fight begins over these three sentimental items, that my son and daughter realize one important thing. They can take the pictures to any drug store and have duplicates made for twenty five dollars. Maybe I ought to leave twenty five dollars in my will, expressly for that purpose!

Here is how Dr. Terry D. Hargrave, puts it, "Often what people fight over (after a loved one dies) has nothing to do with the financial value of the objects. We even attach special meaning to household knickknacks…I have seen brothers go to war over their father's pen. After months of bickering and legal maneuvering, they finally settled the issue by framing the pen and alternating custody every other year."[47]

Why this bizarre behavior over seemingly insignificant material things? I believe it is partly due to the memories represented by those items and the love (or lack of love) that the owner of those things passed down.

In 1965, the Smothers Brothers comedy team recorded their 8th album. The title of the comedy album was, "Mom always liked you best." It was a hilarious skit and very true to life. The fact of the matter is, sometimes truth hurts. The skit, "Mom always liked you best", was funny and popular because it dealt with an issue as old as time itself. That issue is sibling rivalry. I would be willing to bet that central to the war over dad's pen described above, was "who did dad love more?" Here's the thing, children don't necessarily want to be loved equally, but they do deserve to be loved uniquely.

In the end, the things that truly last in life are the love we have experienced and the memories that last for a lifetime. Love (or lack of it) and memories create our core values. They are the most important things we take with us on life's journey. They are also the most important things we pass on to those who follow us.

In his book, <u>The Measure of a Man, a Spiritual Autobiography</u>, Sidney Poitier tells the story about an acting part he turned down. It was early in his acting career. It was a time when he was in the "starving artist" stage of his career. The acting part that Poitier turned down was a part he felt had no strength of character. By turning down that part, Sidney Poitier defined forever his acting career. Here is how Sidney Poitier describes turning down the part. Poitier also describes how Marty Baum, his agent, reacted to the turn down.

Sidney Poitier writes, "It (the acting part) was paying 750 dollars a week. It would have been a nice piece of change."

Marty, Poitier's agent responds.

"Well, I'll tell you what. I don't know what's going on with you, but anybody as crazy as you, I want to handle him."[48]

Marty Baum knew character and values when he saw them. He also had a sense of what an exceptional actor Sidney Poitier would turn out to be.

A famous basketball coach said this. "Be more concerned with your character than your reputation, because your character is what you really are, while your reputation is merely what others think you are.[49]

"The world may be different because I was important in the life of a child." Speaking of coaches, they can be some of the most influential people in our lives. Coach Ken was the most influential coach during my teenage years. I can still hear Coach Ken yelling at us at the end of practice. The yelling came as we were running wind sprints. The wind sprints were always at the end of football or basketball practice. We were already dead tired. He would push us into better shape and endurance by yelling, "What are you saving it for? It's the fourth quarter!"

I have thought of that encouragement often. I didn't appreciate the wisdom of those words as a winded teenager at the end of a long, hot practice. I have, however, learned to appreciate the wisdom of those words as I have grown older. When you think about it, those words of encouragement are especially valid as they apply to our God given talents, our God given money and our God given time on this earth. What are we saving it for, indeed?

Talents, money and time are meant to be spent and not saved. Here is how one enthusiast has put it, "life should NOT be a journey to the grave with the intention of arriving safely in an attractive and well preserved body, but rather to skid in sideways, chocolate in one hand, martini in the other, body thoroughly used up, totally worn out and screaming "WOO HOO what a ride!"[50]

Of course, I fully realize you can take the idea of "WOO HOO" too far, but you can also take our cultural obsession with "health" too far. How about some balance? Sometimes, this is what I want to say to both fast food junkies and heath food junkies. Lighten up! To the fast food junkies I want to say, count the costs of that diet. The costs may be diabetes, obesity and shorter lifespan. To the people obsessed with all things "healthy" I have a word from comedian Redd Foxx. "Health nuts are going to feel stupid someday, lying in the hospital dying of nothing."[51]

What are you saving it for? This question applies equally to the spending of talents, time and money. Let me take them in order.

Our talents are what we are naturally good at. I talked about the use of our talents in Chapter 1 when I spoke of work as vocation or calling. Frederick Buechner has a great definition of vocation or calling. "The place God calls you to, is the place where your deep gladness and the world's deep hunger meet."[52]

So, what are you saving your talents for? Find your gladness and match it with the world's needs? There are a variety of aptitude and personality tests out there that will help you discern how your talents can best be used. Amazingly, you may even find an employer who will pay you to use the God given talents that you have so freely been given by God! Here's a thought. Maybe you can even use those God given talents to start your own business. With your own unique talents, the sky's the limit.

What about money? What are you saving it for? How should I spend my money? Harry Wendt, a teacher and Bible scholar, has one of the best definitions of money I have ever come across. He defines money as "effort, love, and service in a storable, exchangeable form."[53] How can we set our priorities as they relate to money? (Talents measured in storable, exchangeable form.)

Can I make what some might consider a totally outrageous suggestion? What if you were to save ten percent of your money, give away ten percent of your money and spend the remaining eighty percent on your basic needs?

Now I can hear you say, "That's totally impossible!" How can he have the audacity to suggest that I give ten percent of my money away? Then, on top of that, save an additional ten percent of my money? Doesn't he know that I can barely make ends meet as it is?

Here is the truth. "If you can't live on 80 percent of your income, you can't live on one hundred percent either."[54] I realize this is a difficult truth to accept, but I believe it is true.

To put this into some perspective here is an interesting statistic. Did you know that about one sixth of the world's population lives on less than $1 a day? Did you know that 92% of the world's population doesn't have an automobile? Did you know that only 1% of the world's population has a college education or owns a computer?[55]

I share these statistics merely to show you that the idea of wealth, or lack thereof, is a relative concept.

Now, I fully realize that a good portion of the people living on less than a dollar a day live in a cashless, barter economy. It's a harsh reality, but they get by on far less than we can even imagine surviving on. I am not suggesting that in 21st century American society we can live on a dollar a day, but I still want to hold out the challenge to you. How might your life change if you could practice 80-10-10? I have met many people who have managed their lives around the 80-10-10 principle and here is the amazing thing. They seem to have enough.

I do not subscribe to the belief that because we practice giving and saving ten percent we will automatically be "blessed." I realize that some modern day preachers of the "prosperity gospel", (especially ones who are on television selling books) promise you the blessings of health, wealth and happiness. It is presumed by many in the "prosperity gospel" business that health, wealth and happiness will come quicker if you give the 10% away, especially to their ministry.

In contrast to the promises of the "prosperity gospel", I can only promise you two things if you practice the discipline of giving 10% and saving 10%.

Are you ready for them?

Here they are:

1. I promise that you will be 10% poorer, based on what you give away.
2. I promise you will be 10% richer based on what you save for the future.

It may seem an impossible discipline to practice at first. If you want to give this idea a try, you might want to build up to it in stages. The first thing you will need to do is calculate what percentage of your income you save and what percentage of your income you give. Once you find this out, you can then gradually increase it by a half a percent or a full percent per year. The choice is up to you.

Why does this stewardship discipline seem to work for many? I have a very practical answer to that question. I think the 80-10-10 principle works for one simple reason. If a person saves 10% and gives 10%, it stands to reason they will be more aware and careful with the 80% that remains. Simply put, awareness produces good decisions.

Contrast this with the vast majority of people who may know how much they make, but they have no earthly idea how much they spend. The only thing they know for certain is that there is far too much "week" and not enough "pay" left in the term "weekly pay."

My wife and I believe so strongly in this principle that we have included it in our Last Will and Testament. Here is what it says,

> "To our beloved children: the remainder of our assets is passed on to you in hopes that you will use it wisely and generously. Any financial assets remaining can be attributed to two deeply held values. The first value is that we have always tried to live beneath our means as good managers of what God has given us. Secondly, we have tried to live by the principle of giving 10%, saving 10% and spending the rest with joyful thanksgiving. We pass on these gifts and values hoping you may know both the joy of receiving and the joy of giving. We love you! – Mom and Dad"[56]

Allow me to add one additional word on the topic of money. It's an old fashion idea. Some would say it is an outdated idea. It can be a totally effective idea if put into practice. The idea is this. You can't spend what you don't have.

I love this quote, "A credit card is the greatest invention since the wheel. It is able to convert thrift into greed instantly. It makes it possible for all of us to buy things we don't need, with money we don't have, to impress people we don't like."[57]

The title of this chapter quotes Forest Witcraft who said, "The world may be different because I was important in the life of a child".

Kids cannot and should not have everything they want, when they want it. That is a pretty bold statement. However, I believe it is an important value to pass on. This basic value is commonly referred to as "deferred gratification."

My kids probably have two words they heard as children that they vow they will never say to children. They surely don't remember everything they ever asked for, but they do remember hearing a common response from their parents. They would often ask their mom and me for stuff. If you are a parent you know the routine. Why can't we have a horse like the Smith family? Why can't we have a dog like the Jones family? Why can't we go to Disney World like the Brown family? Here is why. Some (horses) they didn't really want. Some (Disney vacations) they did not realize were simply too expensive. Some (dogs) were plainly not good ideas because they were too young to be given the responsibility of caring for a pet.

So here are the two words my kids vow never to say to kids. The words are, "some day." That was the common response my wife and I would make to the myriad of requests coming our way. We would simply say, "some day."

After hearing this response far too many times, one day my daughter said in total exasperation, "Someday means never!"

I guess in some ways she was right. I suppose some things they asked for, they "never" got. Lots of the things they asked for they eventually did get. It's just that they got them later rather than sooner. I suspect that today they would not consider themselves "underprivileged kids", especially by the world's standards. However, I happen to believe that there are benefits in teaching deferred gratification.

> *The Stanford marshmallow experiment was a study on deferred gratification. In the study, a marshmallow was offered to each child. If the child could resist eating the marshmallow, he was promised two instead of one. The scientists analyzed how long each child resisted the temptation of eating the marshmallow, and whether or not doing so had an effect on their future success. The results provided researchers with great insight on the psychology of self-control.*
>
> *Walter Mischel, the designer of the experiment, discovered an unexpected correlation between the results of the marshmallow test, and the success of the children many years later. The first*

follow-up study, in 1988, showed that "preschool children, who delayed gratification longer in the self-imposed delay paradigm, were described more than 10 years later by their parents as adolescents who were significantly more competent." A second follow-up study, in 1990, showed that the ability to delay gratification also correlated with higher SAT scores.[58]

Let's move on to talk about the use of our time. Time is also is meant to be spent. What are you saving it for? Actually, saving time is really an impossible thing to do. We can no more save time than we can stop a sunrise or sunset. The simple fact is you cannot "save time", "waste time" or "stop time." Every last one of us has exactly the same amount of time. The only difference is how we use our allotment. The best we can hope for is to manage, divide or prioritize our time.

This is not a book about time management. There are dozens of them available from lots of sources. What I am most interested in is the use of time. I believe you should "never let yesterday use up too much of today." In Chapter 3, I shared a poem entitled "The Station." The wisdom of this essay captures all the wisdom of "never allow yesterday, to use up today." Time can only be spent in daily denominations.

Here is thought provoking story about time taken from my preaching days...

The devil sends three apprentices on a recruiting mission. They are to bring back as many converts as they can for the devil's kingdom. The devil promises that the apprentice with the most converts will receive a generous promotion in rank.

The first apprentice returns without a single recruit.

"What strategy did you use?" the devil asked.

The first apprentice said, "I told everyone I met that there was no heaven."

The second apprentice returns without a single recruit.

"What strategy did you use?" the devil asked.

The second apprentice said, "I told everyone I met that there was no hell."

The last apprentice returns with a huge number of recruits.

The devil is extremely impressed. "Good work my son, what strategy did you use?" asked the devil.

The third apprentice said, "I told everyone I met that there was a heaven and there was a hell…but that they had plenty of time!"

We all know that the promise of, "we all have plenty of time", is a lie. However, we live as if we have endless amounts of it.

"Life's tragedy is that we get old too soon and wise too late."[59] Here is a story that proves that just because someone has a title or lots of letters behind their name, it does not guarantee they are wiser. It is a story about one of the "no's" I gave to a seminary professor.

I will never forget the months leading up to the birth of our first child. My wife and I were overjoyed at the prospect of a new baby. However, one problem presented itself about four months prior to my son's birth. It had nothing to do with the health of either the baby or the mother.

You see, at that time I was completing my second year of seminary education. The school curriculum suggested completing a Clinical Pastoral Education module prior to my next year of internship. That internship year would require my wife, the new baby and I to move a thousand miles away one month after the baby was due. The new baby was due in late July.

I had a meeting with a seminary professor who was strongly encouraging me to take the Clinical Pastoral Education (C.P.E.) module in June and July. There was one problem. The C.P.E. module was six hours away from my home. It would require me to be six hours away from my home in those last critical days of the pregnancy. To complicate things further is the fact that we lived in a rural setting. Our home was a one hour drive from the hospital.

To make a long story short, I was not about to be six hours away from my wife during the last weeks of the pregnancy. I was not going to miss all of the pre-natal classes offered by the hospital where our son would be born. I explained this to my professor.

"Well, Jack, this is only your first child. What if your wife is expecting your second or third child during the time of an annual church convention? Will you chose not to attend those conventions if you are expecting a future child during those times?"

Keep in mind that there is a significant imbalance in power between a professor and a seminary student, so I judiciously kept my mouth shut. That does not, however, mean that I didn't know what the answer to his question would be. He was describing a choice between attending a church convention and missing the birth of a child? In my value system, the answer to that question is obvious.

How was the issue resolved? I stood my ground. I didn't take the C.P.E. module that summer. I waited to take the module during my fourth year of studies. Everything worked out just fine. I was present at the birth of our first child, and I completed a required C.P.E. module before graduation.

"Stand for something or you will fall for anything." I think the church leader who shared this quote with the adult Sunday school class would have been proud of my decision.

Like the discussion of anniversaries and the second Sunday of Advent earlier in this chapter, there are certain things that take precedence. The birth of a child and an anniversary are such things.

Two and a half years later I was also present at the birth of our daughter. I didn't have a church convention competing with the birth, but if there had been a church convention at the time of my daughter's birth, I know where I would choose to be.

Why do I bring up this story?

Obviously there will be times where our value system conflicts with the value system of another. Earlier in this chapter I shared the story of the two things I would not sacrifice for my work. I would not sacrifice the health of my body or the wellbeing of my family.

"No man on his death bed ever looked up into the eyes of his family and friends and said, I wish I would have spent more time at the office."[60] To be there at the birth and death of a loved one is the greatest privilege we will ever be afforded. Those events take precedence over most other things.

My two sisters and I were privileged to be at my father's bedside the last week of his life. My father endured his last months of battling bone cancer with a kind of quiet dignity. The family spent the last week of my father's life holding his hand, attending to his needs and watching the hospice staff care for him. One day, as he was nearing death, he said something I will never forget. He said with all sincerity, "You are all I've got."

When it comes down to our final hours here on earth, the loving relationships we share with those closest to us become our most cherished possessions. Our loved ones are who we need by our side as we are ushered into the arms of God.

As I wrote this story about attending the birth of my two children and the death of my father, I am painfully reminded that there are other jobs that don't allow that luxury. There are parents who are deployed in the military, persons who work on ships at sea, those whose work is so critical that they can be called to service at any moment. To those people, we owe our deepest gratitude. Their work really does take precedence over many other life events. May their travels be safe and their homecomings joyful.

"100 years from now it will not matter what my bank account was, the sort of house I lived in, or the kind of car I drove, but the world may be different because I was important in the life of a child."

"Live so that your son, when they tell him that he reminds them of you, will stick his chest out and not his tongue."[61]

I have been blessed to be a pastor for 30 plus years. This calling has provided me with income, personal satisfaction and an opportunity to serve others and my community. When the congregation threw me a little party for my retirement, I was deeply grateful. At that party, I gave the following short, farewell speech.

"Dear friends, I am honored and humbled by your outpouring of prayers, cards and well wishes. I only hope that, for the most part, my ministry will be judged to have been faithful to the gospel and to the people I was called to serve. But, with all due respect, as much as I appreciate your outpouring of thanks there are two expressions that mean more to me than all the others combined. I think you will agree when I share them with you.

> The first expression of love came the week I sent out the announcement that I would be retiring. I came into my office one day. On my office desk was a Snickers candy bar, left there by my daughter, Terra. Here is the note I received that week from her.
>
> *Dear Dad,*
>
> *Thank you very much for sharing your well written, well-thought-out letter to the congregation. (The letter announcing my retirement.) That must have been very hard to write, but I think you did an excellent job of expressing your feelings about retirement. I will keep you in my prayers in the coming days.*
>
> *I hope that you receive love and support from the people that you have faithfully served as pastor. I love you very much, and I'm very proud of everything that you do. I'm very proud to call you "Dad."*
>
> *Love, Terra.'*

The second expression I hold dear is a note my son, Nathan, wrote in his card of congratulations. It said,

"Dad,

I admire your many years of service to your congregations and community. I'm proud of your dedication.

Love, Nathan."[62]

If the acid test of a life well lived is that "the world may be different because you were important in the life of a child..."

Judging from my kid's notes, I think I passed the acid test.

QUESTIONS FOR REFLECTION

1. What people have been the most important influences in establishing the values and priorities you hold dear?
2. Can you think of times where those important values were challenged by others? How did you react to those challenges?
3. How "wealthy" was your family in relation to setting values, sharing time, teaching important life lessons to you?
4. Who was the "wealthiest" person materially or spiritually you have ever known?
5. Did you feel rich or poor as you were growing up? Why?

6. Who among adult family or friends would you most aspire to being like?

7. How were money and the issues surrounding money handled in your family?

8. Who among your adult family and friends would you most NOT aspire to being like?

9. Can you think of defining moments in your life where your values and priorities helped you choose one direction versus another? How was that a defining moment?

10. Can you think of children you have been able to affect for the good in your life?

Grandpa Gust Gustafson & Jack - 1966

Ray & Jean Kaczmarek, Kathy & Jack Ottoson,
Jean & Ludwig Ottoson - 1972

Nathan, Kathy, Jack & Terra Ottoson 1986

Jack, Nathan, Kathy and Terra Ottoson at Bullen Jr. High

Terra, safe in Grandpa Ray's arms

Ray & Jack 42" shark, September 8, 2000

Chapter 5

Chapter 5: Summary
<u>"Not everything that is faced can be changed, but nothing can be changed until it is faced."</u>[63]

There is an aphorism (defined as a unique, witty & wise saying) that goes, "Your foot will never get well as long as the horse is still standing on it." I learned many years ago that the way you react to an event may be far more important than the actual event itself. Unfortunately, we too often fixate on those problems in our lives which literally have no solution. We concentrate on ways to "fix" the behavior of others, who we have no control over, yet we ignore fixing our own behavior. "Letting go and letting God" is a path to a much more satisfying life.

<u>"Not everything that is faced can be changed, but nothing can be changed until it is faced."</u>[64]

"Denial ain't just a river in Egypt."[65]

Denial, is the human ability to avoid facing things which are right in front of us. Humans have an amazing capacity to deny those things that are staring us right in the face.

Denial can be used as a defense mechanism, an excuse and a source of who or what to blame. It can also be an explanation. As the chapter title attests, what denial can never do is find a path to change. Change can only begin after the denial is faced.

Recognizing the roots of our behavior doesn't excuse our behavior. In Chapter 3 I quoted Pastor Rick Warren who wrote, "We are products of our past but we don't have to be prisoners of it."[66] His words fit again as we think about denial. Explaining our behavior as a product of our past may answer the why of how we act but it doesn't answer the how leading to change.

Denial. How is it that we humans have the perfect ability to look directly at something and at the same time deny that it is there? I'll give you a perfect example.

Just the other day I was looking in the freezer for a frozen package of potatoes to cook for supper. My wife was certain the package was in the freezer, so I said I would look for it. I was persistent. I was diligent. I took every item off the freezer shelves twice! Finally, in desperation and defeat, I said to Kathy, "I give up. I know the package is there but I simply can't find it."

You guessed it. She found the package on the first try.

"Well, if it had been a snake it would have bitten you, so how could you miss it?" She didn't actually say that, but I know she was thinking it.

In my defense there is a psychological term for what I just experienced. I looked it up. The phenomenon I had just experienced is called "inattentional blindness." It means we are unable to see something, even if it is in plain sight. It happens to us all the time.

We pass by something that is in plain view and we don't notice it. We look for something and we literally cannot see it. In the case of the frozen package of potatoes, I was looking for a package in the shape of a small rectangle. The frozen potatoes came in the form of a large, round bag. I even handled the large round bag of frozen potatoes a number of times in my search for it. My mind passed right over the word potatoes on the outside of the package. My brain never registered what I had right in my hands. I wasn't expecting the package to look the way it did. It should be a rectangular box, not a round bag.

Now, don't tell me you haven't done the same thing? I know you have. How about when you try to switch traffic lanes and hear a loud honk? You may have looked in your rear view mirror. You may have seen the car with your eyes. Somehow the car didn't register in your brain.

Or, when was the last time you drove someplace and don't remember half of the places you passed by? That's inattentional blindness.

This is an especially dangerous problem with automobile drivers who don't "see" motorcycles and bicycles. The principle of inattentional blindness causes the driver to not notice the object. The sad part is that a motorcycle or a bicycle always loses against an auto. A person on a motorcycle or a bicycle has to learn to expect the unexpected. When I ride a bicycle, I always assume a driver isn't looking for me and does not fully see me.

If you want some interesting reading, look up inattentional blindness and discover for yourself the studies that document how we can literally overlook things that are right in front of our eyes.

Sorry, I have strayed from the chapter title, "Not everything that is faced can be changed, but nothing can be changed until it is faced."

Like the phenomenon of "inattentional blindness", there are good explanations about why we may not see certain things. However, a person or an event can break us out of inattentional blindness.

My wife handed the bag of frozen potatoes to me with an exasperated look on her face. The person who we cut off in traffic, honks the horn to get our attention.

Inattentional blindness is really not the type of denial that the chapter title addresses. I would place "inattentional blindness" more in the category of involuntary reflexes. Think coughs, sneezes and shivers.

No, the denial I am thinking about is not about what our minds do not register. Rather, the denial I am thinking of is related to seeing things maybe a little too clearly. We see things that we would rather not see or accept. We choose to avoid, rather than confront and change. Sometimes, we choose to see and ignore these things to our own peril.

In his book, <u>The Road Less Traveled,</u> M. Scott Peck describes four tools for dealing with human suffering. One of those tools is "dedication to truth." He says, truth telling "is indeed a never-ending burden of self-discipline, which is why most people opt for a life of very limited honesty and openness and relative closedness, hiding themselves and their maps from the world."[67]

One way of being "dedicated to the truth" is the willingness and ability to confront denial both in ourselves and others. It is the only way through suffering and into change. "Problems do not go away. They must be worked through or else they remain, forever a barrier to the growth and development of the spirit."[68]

Helena, (not her real name) was a kindly woman. She was always one of the first worshippers out the door after church. I was an intern pastor at the time. I took a liking to this frail, older woman. My keen sense of smell noticed the distinct smell of alcohol whenever I would greet Helena at the door. Keep in mind that this was at 10 a.m. in the morning.

I shared my suspicions that Helena might have a drinking problem with my supervising pastor. He never took my observations seriously. Actually, maybe he didn't want to take them seriously. If he had taken them seriously, he would have told me to do something about the observations. Both of us were in denial about Helena's problem.

Months later, Helena ended up in the hospital. The diagnosis was somewhat mysterious. She had anemia from loss of blood. After a few days in the hospital, Helena died.

Her husband happened to be an officer in the military. As the spouse of an officer, Helena was accorded a military funeral with full honors. She also had the right to be buried in a national military cemetery. I presided at that burial. It was all so proper. It came with lots of pomp and circumstance. I helped bury a secret that day.

I can still remember my confusion, anger and grief at the loss of Helena. She didn't seem to be that sick. The official doctor's report said she died of a bleeding ulcer, but I knew the truth. Helena had died from abuse of the cheapest and most available drug in America, alcohol.

To my supervisor's credit, he recommended that I attend an "open" Alcoholics Anonymous" meeting. An open AA meeting is one where anyone from the community can attend to learn about addiction. It was there, for the first time, that I was able to talk about my anger, confusion and grief over Helena's death. They understood. Everyone at that meeting had walked through that valley. At that meeting I began the journey of learning more about this insidious disease.

The first step of Alcoholics Anonymous is, "We admitted we were powerless over alcohol - that our lives had become unmanageable."[69] The first step in recovery begins with breaking through denial.

In over ten years of volunteering as a chaplain at two separate substance abuse treatment centers I have listened to dozens of 5th step "confessions." Trust me, I have heard my share of denial. Here are some examples of some of the denials I have heard.

"I couldn't be an alcoholic…because I never miss any days at work."

"I don't have a substance abuse problem…because my family never complains about me."

"I never…drink and drive."

Here is my personal favorite, "I can stop at any time."

The list of denials goes on and on.

When all is said and done, here is the simplest and best definition of substance abuse that I have ever heard. "If your drinking (or drug abuse) causes you problems, then you have a problem with drinking (or drug abuse)."

Why is it so hard to break through denial? I believe the biggest roadblock is one powerful word, "powerlessness." After all, no one wants to be powerless. The highest values in our society are strength, independence and being in control of our own destiny. No one wants to consider themselves "powerless."

To face denial means confronting our own denial and the denial of others. Let's face it, few people like being confronted or initiating confrontation. Even if it can save a life, confrontation is extremely hard work. But, the concept of "raising the bottom" by confrontation can be effective. In the language of drug treatment it is called intervention.

Here is how one source describes intervention. "With the assistance of a well put together drug abuse intervention, the drug abuser is able to sit back and take a look at their addiction through their family and friends' eyes. The decision to hold a drug abuse intervention can be a painful one, but it is less painful than watching a loved one being controlled by a substance without facing their own life reality. Many loved ones do not want to force their addicted member to lose control or feel as if they are being attacked, but it is very important for the addict to see what they are doing to those close to them."[70]

Would an intervention have worked with Helena? Unfortunately, I will never know the answer to that question. It will remain both a mystery and a regret of mine for as long as I live. Years after her death I would read an article titled,

"Killing with Kindness." It is exactly what we do by maintaining the silent and safe position of denial.

I have one caution here. Interventions are not for the faint of heart. Even with the collaboration of a professional, family members and friends, an intervention may not work. The question is, how long do you want to live with the denial? The pain of not doing something may be greater than the pain of doing something, so seek out the help. It may be a lifesaver.

There is another place where we humans exhibit denial and blindness. It is so deeply ingrained in us that it may take a lifetime to understand. It is attitude. I am reminded again of Dr. M. Scott Peck's words quoted earlier, "most people opt for a life of very limited honesty and openness and relative closedness, hiding themselves and their maps from the world."

French-Cuban writer Anais Nin puts it best, "we do not see things as they are; we see them as we are." If we are serious about facing our own denial on the path to change, we would do well to begin with how and why we see the world the way it is. It may serve as a window on that path of change. The first step may be to face our own pre-conceived, pre-judged, notions of things. Our understanding or reaction to the world may say more about us, than it does about the world.

There is a concept in social psychiatry called "attribution theory." Simply put, "our attributions, whether correct or incorrect, are more responsible than objective reality for how we think, what we feel, and how we behave. Studies have shown, for example, that we commonly attribute greater warmth, sexiness, and other desirable traits to good-looking people than to homely people, and behave toward them accordingly."[71]

To be honest, an old story illustrates this better than any psychology textbook.

From Abesville to Reedsville

A farmer was working in his field one day when he saw a man driving in a U-Haul truck. The man pulled over to the side of the road to ask the farmer a question. The driver explained that he was moving from Abesville to Reedsville, but had lost his way. The farmer gave him the necessary directions to get to Reedsville. The driver of the truck then asked the farmer one more question, "I've never been to Reedsville before. I was wondering, are the people friendly there?" The farmer asked the man whether he had found the people in Abesville to be friendly. The driver responded, "The people in Abesville were the friendliest group of people I have ever met. There wasn't a person there that I didn't care for." The farmer smiled and said, "I reckon you'll find the people of Reedsville to be every bit as friendly." With that, the driver thanked the farmer for his help and drove off.

> The very next day the farmer was back working the same field and once again a driver in a U-Haul truck pulled over to talk to him. This man had lost his way and began to explain that he was in the process of moving from Abesville to Reedsville. So once again the farmer gave the driver the necessary directions. Then this driver too explained that he had never been to Reedsville and that he too was wondering if the people were friendly there. So, the farmer asked him whether he had found the people in Abesville to be friendly. The man responded, "The people in Abesville were the least friendly group of people I have ever met. I didn't care for a one of them." The farmer thought for a moment and shook his head. He said to the man, "I'm afraid you will find the people in Reedsville to be just about the same way."

That powerful story, "From Abesville to Reedsville", was printed in a counseling center's newsletter. I read it years ago. It remains true with a capital "T."[72]

The writer of the article explains that there are at least two possible interpretations of the story. The first possible interpretation is that the second driver may have, in fact, experienced hurt by the people of Abesville, but the farmer was wise enough to know that unless this justifiable hurt and anger was dealt with, it would be difficult for the man to experience the friendliness of the people in Reedsville.

The second possible interpretation is that the farmer was wise enough to know that to a large degree we create the tenor of our own emotional universe. The prejudices and projections we bring into new relationships help shape what those relationships will be.

No matter which interpretation you choose, the fact remains that our attitude directly affects how we see and interact with the world.

I would like to share a story from our own family. It illustrates attitudes and how they can dramatically affect impressionable children.

When my son was 6 and my daughter was 3, we made a major relocation. We moved into a quaint, but small, two-story house. Fortunately, we didn't own lots of furniture, but my son did sleep in a rather large bunk bed. The bunk bed was hand made by his grandpa. Unfortunately, the bunk bed was too tall to assemble in his tiny upstairs bedroom. The sloped ceiling would mean that only the bottom bunk could be used to sleep in because the top bunk was right up against the ceiling. Trying to create the most positive construction on the problem, we explained it this way to our son. We told our son that if he had friends over, rather than sleep on the upper bulk we could place the mattresses on the bedroom floor. Both he and his friends could sleep like "China men." (Forgive us here. My wife and I know all Chinese people do not sleep on the floor! We were just trying to make lemonade out of lemons.)

When my 3-year-old daughter heard about this arrangement she began crying inconsolably. After she calmed down enough to be understood through her sobbing, she declared with crocodile tears in her eyes, "but I want to sleep like China men too!"

Isn't it amazing how she attributed sleeping on the floor as a privilege? Why? It is because we had framed the problem of the smaller house, with the smaller bedroom, with the sloped ceiling, with no room to fit the bunk bed, as both an opportunity and an adventure.

Our 3-year-old didn't say to us, "Why did you have to move into such a small house where our furniture won't even fit?" No, instead she attributed sleeping on the floor as a privilege that she also wanted to experience. My wife and I had framed the problem into an opportunity. We made an adventure out of it. We had made lemonade out of lemons, and our 3-year-old daughter wanted a taste of that lemonade.

I recall that we did, in fact, allow our daughter to move her mattress to the floor so she could try sleeping like a China man. However, she soon tired of this arrangement and we moved the mattress back onto her bed frame.

As I have mentioned earlier in this book, one of my motivations in writing this book is to leave behind something of value to my children. Maybe the words, ideas and wisdom learned from my mistakes can make their lives a little better? Eleanor Roosevelt said, "You must learn from the mistakes of others. You can't possibly live long enough to make them all yourself."

Here is a confession about my negative attitudes and prejudices. Despite our best intentions, my wife and I have left behind both our positive values AND our negative attitudes and prejudices. There is no reason to list all of our negative attitudes and prejudices here, but the older I get, the more I examine the negative attitudes and prejudices that have blocked my own growth. Sometimes, after I say or think something that is narrow minded and judgmental, I ask myself, "Jack, where did that come from?" The answer is usually not from any objective experience I have had. Usually, it is from an attitude or prejudice passed down or taught to me. Occasionally, it is a single negative experience that I generalize to a whole group of people.

About the only thing I can say about these negative attitudes and prejudices is that my kids will just have to recognize and sort out these passed down negative attitudes and prejudices for themselves. I'm afraid their only other choice is to go to the parent store and pick out a better set of parents.

But, what if my kids go to the parent store to pick out a new set of parents? Guess what? That new set of parents will come equipped with a whole unique set of negative attitudes and prejudices! So, there's no denying it. We passed on the good as well as the bad. All we can really hope for is that the good somehow outweighs the bad.

The main point is this. Attitude can make all the difference.

Here are some quotes from others who have addressed the importance of attitude in life…

"The greatest discovery of my generation is that human beings can alter their lives by altering their attitudes of mind. Be willing to have it so. Acceptance of what has happened is the first step to overcoming the consequences of any misfortune."[73]

"The longer I live, the more I realize the impact of attitude on life. Attitude, to me, is more important than facts. It is more important than the past, than education, than money, than circumstances, than failures, than successes, than what other people think or say or do. It is more important than appearance, giftedness or skill. It will make or break a company, a church, a home. The remarkable thing is we have a choice every day regarding the attitude we will embrace for that day. We cannot change our past... we cannot change the fact that people will act in a certain way. We cannot change the inevitable. The only thing we can do is play on the one string we have, and that is our attitude. I am convinced that life is 10% what happens to me and 90% how I react to it. And so it is with you. We are in charge of our attitudes."[74]

"You have two choices today: be happy, act happy."[75]

"Don't listen to those who weep and complain for their disease is contagious."[76]

"I have found that most people are about as happy as they make up their mind to be."[77]

Mahatma Ghandi once traveled a long distance to give a lecture. After the lecture, a woman came to him begging him to lecture her son about the dangers of eating too much sugar.

"Master Ghandi, please tell my son not to eat so much sugar!"

Instead of taking the son aside, Ghandi asked the mother to bring the son back in two weeks. That is when he was scheduled to return to that town.

She wasn't happy about the delay.

"Master Ghandi, can you not tell him now?"

Ghandi was firm and again asked the woman to bring the lad back in two weeks.

What could she do but follow his instructions?

After two weeks, Ghandi returned to the same village. This time he did take the son aside to explain the dangers of eating too much sugar. The mother was pleased, but asked Ghandi,

"Master Ghandi, why didn't you tell my son not to eat sugar when you were here two weeks ago?

Ghandi replied, "Because, my dear woman, I did not yet know how difficult it would be to stop eating sugar."

The most difficult thing to face and change in life is <u>not</u> circumstances but attitude. The roots of our attitudes are diverse and complicated, but those roots must be discovered and dealt with if we are serious about growth and change.

Fr. Mike was my supervisor during the hospital rotations of Clinical Pastoral Education. Rarely did students enjoy writing up daily journals, and I was no exception. Fr. Mike's observations and comments in the margins of those journal pages were often well worth the pain of keeping the daily journals in the first place. A particularly powerful insight was written in the margin of my journal on September 10, 1979. I have kept that journal page for 33 years.

Here is what I wrote in my journal that day,

"I'm confused as to just how I can be more open with people. For one thing, the way I have related to people in the past was viewed by some as being open. I also was 'comfortable' and 'loved' with the old system."

Here is Fr. Mike's hand written, enlightened, response in the journal's margin.

"Growth=Change"
"Change=Loss of Old"
"Loss=Grief"
"Grief=Pain"
"Growth=Pain"[78]

There it is. These are the two biggest roadblocks to change. They are denial & pain.

I have received lots of compliments about the current message on our phone answering machine. Here is the message, "Hello, you have reached Jack and Kathy Ottoson. Well, actually you have reached Jack and Kathy's message machine. But, your call is very important to us, so please leave a message at the beep. We'll return your call as soon as possible. **Please go out and make it a great day today!**"

I think there is a simple reason that people like that message, especially the last sentence. The message reinforces the idea that we all have the power to go out and make it a great day.

Let's face it, you can't do anything about the weather today. Let's face it, you can't do anything about the traffic today. Let's face it, you can't do anything about the attitude of your co-worker today. But YOU are in control of YOUR attitude today and that can make all the difference in the world!

Contrast this with the sarcastic attitude of a bumper sticker I saw recently. It proclaimed, "The more you complain, the longer God lets you live."[79]

What kind of day will you make it today? How can your attitude make it a better day?

One of my favorite prayers is entitled, "a prayer for growing old gracefully." I hope you enjoy it.

"Lord, thou knowest better than I know myself that I am growing older and will someday be old. Keep me from being talkative and particularly from the fatal habit of thinking I must say anything on every subject and on every occasion. Release me from craving to straighten out everybody's affairs. Keep my mind from the recital of endless details; give me wings to come to the point. I ask for grace enough to listen to the tales of other's pains. Help me to endure them with patience. But, seal my lips with my own aches and pains. They are increasing and my love of rehearsing them becomes sweeter as the years go by. Teach me the glorious lesson that occasionally it is possible that I may be mistaken. Keep me reasonably sweet. I do not want to be a saint, some of them are so hard to live with—but a sour old woman (or man) is one of the crowning works of the devil. Make me thoughtful, but not moody, helpful, but not bossy. With my vast store of wisdom it seems a pity not to use it all but thou knowest I want a few friends at the end.[80]

As if the prayer above isn't challenging enough, here are just a couple of more quotes for you to consider.

"Remember, there is never a simple answer to a complex question.[81]

"For every complex problem, there is a solution that is simple, neat and wrong."[82]

So, we return to the chapter title. "Not everything that is faced can be changed, but nothing can be changed until it is faced."

I would like to close with more words of wisdom from M. Scott Peck, "Mental health is an ongoing process of dedication to reality at all costs!...Examination of the world without is never as personally painful as examination of the world within, and it is certainly because of the pain involved in a life of genuine self-examination that the majority steer away from it... Entering psychotherapy (or I might add any self-examination process) is an act of the greatest courage."[83]

To change and grow means to face denial. To change and grow means we must face our tendency to procrastinate, to avoid, and to deny our need for growth and change.

To change and grow means we must face our own attitudes which cling to us as tenaciously as our own skin.

To change and grow means to face the inevitable pain that comes with change.

To change and grow should be celebrated. It's just like birthdays, the older you get the more you dislike them. But, if you don't like birthdays, just think of the alternatives.

QUESTIONS FOR REFLECTION

1. Can you think of a time where you maintained a stance of fierce denial?
2. Who are the Helenas in your life? Can you think of ways to intervene for change? Who would you need to collaborate with to make change happen?

3. To what extent do you agree or disagree with "Attribution Theory"?
4. What is true about the "Abesville to Reedsville" story?
5. In your lifetime, what changes or growth have been hardest for you to experience? How did you accomplish and navigate through the growth and change?
6. How can "dedication to the truth" and "courage" help us?
7. What truths about growing old are hardest for you to face?
8. What would you add to the truths of this chapter?
9. If you could pick one way to change and grow right now, what would it be?
10. What books have etched their ideas and truths on your life?

Chapter 6

Chapter 6: Summary

"A friend is a push when you're stopped, a word when you're lonely, a guide when you're searching, a smile when you're sad, and a song when you're glad."[84]

This is a chapter exploring the importance of friendship and support along life's journey. A true friendship can provide us with the compassion, support and perspective we can never get on our own. It may be one of the simplest secrets to a happy life.

"A friend is a push when you're stopped, a word when you're lonely, a guide when you're searching, a smile when you're sad, and a song when you're glad."[85]

Friendships may be one of the simplest secrets to a happy and satisfying life. I mentioned in Chapter 4 that there is strong evidence that "over the fence" counseling may be as effective as paid, professional counseling when it comes to dealing with the daily stresses and strains of life. Here are two thoughts that illustrate what I mean.

"It's the friends you can call up at 4 AM that matter."[86]

"We need to have people who mean something to us, people to whom we can turn knowing that being with them is coming home."[87]

How important it is for all of us to have friends we can count on! We need to have friends we can turn to, even at 4 AM. We need to have friends who will lend us a listening ear when we need one. We need to have friends who are honest with us, even when we may not like what they have to say.

Garrison Keillor is a master weaver of tales. In his story, "Storm Home", he describes what it is like to have a place of refuge. Keillor, who grew up in Anoka, MN, knows firsthand about the sudden, ferocious nature of Minnesota blizzards. His story tells how children from the rural areas were assigned a "storm home" in town. When the roads were unsafe for busses to take students back to the rural areas, the "storm home" would serve as a safe place to stay. Garrison's fictional "storm home" was the home of the Kruegers. He never actually stayed at his "storm home", but it did loom large in his imagination. He writes…

> *Blizzards aren't the only storms you know and not necessarily the worst thing that can happen to a child. And I often dreamed about going and knocking on their door. And she'd open the door and she'd say,*

'Ah, it's you! I knew you'd come someday. I'm so glad to see you. Won'tcha come on in, get out of those wet clothes. Come on into the kitchen. Sit down. I'll make you some hot chocolate. Would ja like an oatmeal cookie or sumpthin?'

...I never did go there. We didn't have any blizzards that came during the day that year or the year after that. They were all convenient blizzards. Evening and weekend blizzards. But they (the Kruegers) became a big part of my imagination and I always thought that I could go to the Kruegers. And I didn't, I guess, because all of my troubles were bearable troubles. But, I'm certain that they were more bearable for imagining that the Kruegers were there. My storm home."[88]

Did you hear that! "I am certain that they (my troubles) were more bearable for imagining that the Kruegers were there."

Ahhh...the comfort of knowing you have a storm home. That's the power of true friendship. Simply knowing you have a friend that you **could** call at 4 AM makes all the difference in the world. How many of our problems would become "more bearable" by just knowing we had a "storm home" friend to go to?

"During his training, Dr. Sigmund Freud encountered a patient suffering from paralysis and an inability to speak her native

German language. Freud's colleague, Josef Breuer, discovered that if he hypnotized her, she would talk of things she did not remember in the conscious state, and afterwards her symptoms were relieved -- thus it was called "the talking cure."[89]

Now, I fully realize that there are serious psycho-social problems that need the attention of the best people our medical profession has to offer. In serious cases, a good friend needs to be discerning and supportive in directing someone to the best professional help available. In addition, a friend needs to know their limits. They need to understand when they are "in over their head." Having said all this, isn't it amazing how powerful the simple gift of talking, listening and empathy can be? Sometimes people just need a "storm home."

A friend can also be a push when you are stopped. Sometimes, "a friend is one who tells you what you need to know, not what you want to hear."[90]

Is it any wonder that professionals in countless fields have created associations? The most common purpose of these groups is to offer mutual support, continuing education and licensing/certification. In many ways these associations allow us to hear what we need to hear from others who walk in the same profession as we do.

In 1980 I was ordained as a Lutheran pastor. Soon after my ordination I heard the following quote from a colleague and mentor of mine. He was assistant to our District President. He had many years of pastoral experience. Here is the quote he shared,

"There is no special honor in being called to the preaching ministry, there is only special pain. The pulpit calls those anointed to it as the sea calls its sailors and like the sea, it batters and bruises and does not rest. To preach, to really preach, is to die naked a little at a time and to know each time you do it, that you must do it again."[91]

The power of the internet allowed me to research the original writer of those words. During the search for the author, I also happened on a web/blog site that featured the exact quote on the web/blog's front page. The web/blog's site encouraged readers to make comments about the quote. Here is a very entertaining comment about the quote.

"Man, that will weed out those who are just looking for a job!"[92]

Does the quote my mentor shared sound overly dramatic? Does the quote sound overly negative? The quote may ignore the many joys in the preaching ministry, but every preacher knows the kernel of truth behind those words of Pastor Bruce W. Thielmann.

Over the years I have been blessed by my association with colleagues of every denomination. We have formed "miniature associations" around the study of Sunday's scripture lessons. We have formed associations around our mutual need for friendship and collegial support. We have formed associations around our need to serve the local community. We have even formed associations around the love of a sport, like racquetball or golf.

No matter what the "original" intention of the group, here's what is certain: sooner or later the group would eventually share the joys and pains of the vocation we call pastoral ministry. Whatever the "original" purpose of the group, the fact remains that we all needed to talk about those joys and pains. Those joys and pains are an essential part of being called into the service of God and others. As a result of those associations, I have developed some deep, lifelong friendships. It is no exaggeration to say that those groups made ministry more bearable and more joyful.

I think at the heart of professional associations is the basic human need to understand and to be understood. This is especially true in the "caring" professions. The "storm home" analogy is a fitting one here. People in the "caring" professions need the affirmation, understanding and support of those who know "what it is like" to be a _____. (Fill in here the caring profession of your choice.)

But, it is not just a need of people in "professions." All workers in any pursuit need the understanding and support of those who they work side by side with. This is the reason for that drink or dinner after work. This is the reason for the work bowling league or the work awards ceremony or the work picnic. Well, you get the picture. Think of the TV sitcom "Cheers": "you wanna be where everybody knows your name."

During my working years, I never failed to read a bi-monthly magazine column. It was titled "Pastor Loci." The column was written by a pastor, for the ears of pastors. With unfailing wit, sarcasm and understanding, Pastor Steven L. McKinley explored the joys and sadness of pastoral ministry. I have a file brimming with the gems of his written columns. Here is what he wrote in a column called, "Staying the Hammers."

"We went to a movie on a Saturday afternoon. A quote came up on the screen that blew me away. 'A man works his whole life in a glass factory. One day he feels like picking up a hammer.'

I repeated the quote to a number of pastor friends in the following weeks. To a person, they got a little sad in the face and nodded. They knew what this quote was all about. They had been eyeing the hammer themselves."[93]

Pastor McKinley went on to write a rousing column urging all members of our church denomination to find ways to affirm one another, support one another, cheer for one another and celebrate one another. He concluded, "If we do that, the hammers will stay in the closets where they belong."[94]

A good deal of the responsibility for finding the right associations, the most helpful support system, and the best friendships, rests entirely on us. As important as friends are in our life, they don't automatically show up on our doorstep. The modern term for finding the support we need is "intentionality." We have to go out looking for it. If it is important, and it truly is, then it will take some searching on our part.

In 1996, I walked into the office of Pastor Paul. I was a new pastor in town. I had been called to develop a new congregation for my church denomination. In my previous community, I had developed a new congregation. Now I was not only in a new community, but I was in a whole new state. Pastor Paul had successfully developed a congregation for his denomination, and I wanted to get to know him. We immediately hit it off. After all, we had traveled down similar roads. We had a great deal in common. Paul invited me to a weekly prayer/accountability group. It was comprised of three pastors who met for two hours weekly.

No "miniature association" I have ever been a part of was more powerful and supportive as that "prayer/accountability" group. I thank God to this day for the invitation of my friend, Pastor Paul.

From 1996 until my retirement in 2009, I attended that weekly prayer/accountability group. In those years the group was usually made up of 4 pastors. It was an inter-denominational group and we committed 2-4 hours a week to the group. We were dedicated to prayer, listening and holding each other accountable for the week ahead.

In that length of time, the group of 4 changed many times. Pastors moved on to other communities and other calls. When that happened, the group would discuss the names of pastors we knew who would be strengthened by, and in turn, bring strength to the group.

After prayer and discussion, the group would appoint one of the group members to invite the new pastor to participate. The new person would be entirely free to "try out" the prayer/accountability group before they made a weekly commitment to the group. Paul and I were fortunate to be in the group for thirteen years prior to my retirement in 2009. He still remains a close friend, fishing buddy and faithful participant in the group.

As I mentioned, the group normally would meet for 2-4 hours to share their prayer requests, concerns from the past week, and their plans for the future. There were times when most of the time would be taken up by one or two members of the group. I was always amazed at the sensitivity and discernment of the group in this regard. We always seemed able to give the right amount of time to the group member who needed more of the group's time. Group members would naturally yield time to the member who needed more listening time from others that week.

While every week was unique, we did follow a core discipline of questions. Here are the important questions we would ask each other.

1. What is your stress level on a scale of 1-10?
2. What was your "joy in ministry" this past week?

3. Did you get your day off this week?
4. What should the group pray for and hold you accountable to in the next week?

Did the group work?

Absolutely!

Why?

I believe the following were secrets to the success and power of this group:

a. Denominational differences were less important than faithfulness to God's call.
b. Each member of the group held those hours of the week in high priority and committed to attending faithfully.
c. Things shared in the group were treated with strict confidentiality.
d. We cared about each other and respected our unique gifts.
e. We were not afraid to hold a member's "feet to the fire" on something that the group member had identified as important. When a group member asked to be held accountable for doing or acting in a certain way, we would do just that. (i.e.: Did you make that contact with Mary or John this week? How is that change of diet going? Did you say no to someone or something this week?)

Without question it was one of the most supportive and caring groups I have been a part of in my 30 years of ministry. The group was originally started by two pastors who sensed a need for collegiality, prayer and support. There is no perfect number of participants. Four committed participants seemed to be just the right size for our group. That size allowed opportunity for all to share in a 2-3 hour time frame.

Good solid friendships can act as mirrors. Good solid friendships can invite us to grow. Good solid friendships can teach us things about ourselves we could never learn on our own. Here are a few quotes that reinforce the idea of friendship as a mirror.

"If you hate a person, you hate something in him that is part of yourself. What isn't part of ourselves doesn't disturb us."[95]

"It is a very common human inclination (projection) to dislike in others what we cannot accept in ourselves."[96] An old Dutch Proverb declares, "Our faults irritate us most when we see them in others."

If these insights are true, then Shakespeare's words are true for the ages. "A friend is one who knows you as you are, understands where you have been, accepts what you have become, then gently allows you to grow."[97]

In a most profound way, the group I just described above, practiced love. Let me explain.

Writers, poets, moviemakers, songwriters and many others have sold us on a romanticized version of the word 'love'. Allow me to introduce you to another definition of 'love'.

> "In the Christian sense, love is not primarily an emotion but an act of will. When Jesus tells us to love our neighbors, he is not telling us to love them in the sense of responding to them with a cozy emotional feeling. You can as well produce a cozy emotional feeling on demand as you can a yawn or a sneeze. On the contrary, he is telling us to love our neighbors in the sense of being willing to work for their well-being even if it means sacrificing our own well-being to that end, even if it means just leaving them alone. Thus in Jesus' terms we can love our neighbors without necessarily liking them. In fact liking them may stand in the way of loving them by making us overprotective sentimentalists instead of reasonably honest friends…
>
> …This does not mean that liking may not be a part of loving, only that it doesn't have to be. Sometimes liking follows on the heels of loving. It is hard to work for somebody's well-being very long without coming in the end to rather like him too."[98]

Do you see the amazing contrast between this version of "love" and the definition of "love" we are "sold" by our contemporary culture and media? This definition of "love" releases us from sentimentality to action. Our modern era has both narrowed and cheapened the English word "love." Actually, the English word, "serve", might be closer to Jesus' command to "love your neighbor as yourself."[99]

In another place, Jesus said, "This I command you, to love one another."[100]

In the quote above, Frederick Buechner has it exactly right. "Cozy emotional feelings" cannot be commanded. On the other hand, love, seen as an act of will, can be commanded. This kind of love seeks the highest and best for the family, the friend and the neighbor.

What a freeing way to look at love! I may not like the way the other talks. I may not like the way the other dresses. I may not like the way the other acts. But love (service), compels me to work for their well-being just as I would want the other to work for my well-being.

Friendships invite us to grow. That is why I say the prayer/accountability group practiced the concept of "love." To practice love means to hold the other accountable to growth that comes with change.

The prayer/accountability group was practicing what countless self-help groups have discovered. Growth comes with change, and growth that comes from change is far more achievable with the support of others.

It's not like others in the group were forcing us to change. No. As a matter of fact, each member of the group identified where he or she wanted to change. Each member of the group invited the others in the group to hold them accountable. Then, all the prayer/accountability group had to do was remind the group member of what he or she had identified as an issue for accountability in the first place. It was simple, profound and life changing.

To use a common example, think of going to your dentist or doctor.

When are you most motivated to take the best care of your teeth? That's right, just before you have a dental appointment. Why? Because you know you will be held accountable for the ways you have cared for your teeth.

When are you most motivated to take those few pounds off that seemed to sneak up on you? That's right, when you know you have to step on that scale during your next doctor's checkup.

The power of accountability can be a powerful motivator in friendships. If we are courageous enough to invite our friends to hold us accountable, we can grow in physical, mental and spiritual wellbeing. Friends can make all the difference.

Shakespeare's words are true, "a friend accepts what you have become, then gently allows you to grow."

We've talked about the invitation of growth, but let's back up to the first part--acceptance. Acceptance and change are not opposites. Remember that poster I mentioned hanging in my college dorm room? "Accept me as I am, so I may learn what I can become." Acceptance and growth may just be different sides of the same coin.

I recently heard a mother describe a bad day her pre-teen daughter had experienced. Mom said her daughter came home in a grumpy mood which was totally out of character for her daughter. Her daughter's usual demeanor was upbeat and bubbly. Try as mom might, she couldn't get her daughter to talk about her day. What had happened in the day to change her child's usual bright disposition? The daughter simply said, "I don't want to talk about it."

The next morning the daughter came to breakfast exhibiting her normal cheerful demeanor. There had obviously been a mood change from the previous day so mom simply said, "Wow, you seem to be in a good mood today!"

The daughter responded with a wisdom well beyond her years. The daughter said:

"Mom, I figured out that your friends bring both good things and bad things to you. You just have to decide whether you are going to take the whole package."[101]

That's pretty mature insight for a pre-teen girl. Friends do bring both good and bad.

It reminds me of one of the most helpful theological insights from my seminary days. The insight is summarized in four simple Latin words. "Simul justus et peccator."[102] The literal translation is: "simultaneously justified and sinner." It is the insight that the pre-teen girl embraced that day.

What was the insight of that pre-teen girl? "Friends bring both good things and bad things to you." Our friends are a package deal, just as we are a package deal. We have both good and bad wrapped up in us. We are never just righteous. We are never just sinner. We are always, and forever, both saint and sinner at the same time.

Ponder this insight for a moment: "Every saint has a past. Every sinner has a future."[103]

It is an insight similar to that of the pre-teen girl. We are a package deal. As humans we are like a half-baked cake. We are not just people with a past. We are people with a future. It's the same with our friends. Our friends come to us as a package. We come to our friends as a package. The truth is, no package is perfect.

Or, is it?

There is another quote by Jesus that baffles my mind (and minds of many others)

At the end of the Sermon on the Mount Jesus says, "You, therefore, must be perfect, as your heavenly Father is perfect."[104]

Okay, you say -- I was willing to follow you on this love/service business. It even makes a little sense, but "perfection"? Now wait just a minute!

That is exactly my reaction the many times I have read those words from Matthew Chapter 5. What could they possibly mean? I certainly am far from perfect and so are my friends. What can the admonition to "be perfect" mean?

Here are some insights from the noted and brilliant scholar, Fred Craddock. These words have helped me understand Matthew, Chapter 5. He says:

> "It helps to attend more carefully to the word "perfect." The word does not mean morally flawless but rather mature, complete, full grown, not partial. Luke uses the word to speak of fruit *maturing* (8:14) and a course being *finished* (13:32). John uses it to describe the *fully realized* unity of Jesus' followers (17:23) and James employs the same word to characterize works as the *completion* of faith (2:22). Paul's favorite use of the word is to portray the quality of *maturity* among Christians (I Cor. 2:6; Eph. 4:13; Phil. 3:12, 15).

However, this command to be perfect comes most clearly into focus and into the realm of reasonable expectation when viewed within its context. First, the call to perfection comes within a discussion of relationships. Second, Jesus rejects for his followers relationships that are based on the double standard of love for the neighbor and hatred for the enemy. The flaw in such relationships is that they are entirely determined by the other person: the one who is friendly is treated as a friend; the one who behaves as an enemy is an object of hatred; the one who speaks is spoken to; the one who spurns is spurned.

Third, Jesus says that one's life is not to be determined by friend or foe but by God, who relates to all not on the basis of their behavior or attitude toward God but according to God's own nature, which is love. God does not react, but acts out of love toward the just and unjust, the good and the evil. God is thus portrayed as perfect in relationships, that is, complete: not partial but impartial. God's perfection in this context is, therefore, love offered without partiality.

Jesus calls on his followers to be children of God in this same quality. "You, therefore, must be perfect, as your heavenly Father is perfect." In other words, you must love without partiality, as God does. Thus understood, perfection is not only possible but actually realized whenever and wherever our relationships come under the reign of God."[105]

Remember Shakespeare's words? "A friend… gently allows you to grow."

Hear the scholar's words again, "this command to be perfect comes most clearly into focus…within a discussion of relationships."

Hmmm, that sounds like friendships to me.

Oh, now I get it. What if we used the English word "mature" for perfect? When we use "mature" as it relates to our life and our relationships, it throws a whole different light on the words of Jesus.

We are called to "maturity" and our friends can be an integral part of helping us grow into the most full and mature…Mary, John or Beth… we can possibly be.

In Professor Craddock's essay we hear that word again, love. "In other words, you must love without partiality, as God does." Doesn't that sound a lot like what the pre-teen girl said? "Friends bring both good things and bad things to you. You just have to decide whether you are going to take the whole package." Love means taking the whole package, without partiality.

It is impossible for me to write about friendship without talking about marriage. While marriage involves a much deeper commitment than many friendships, it goes without saying that a good marriage should have qualities of a good friendship.

A search of the internet reveals numerous studies that show that the health and longevity of married persons far exceeds those of single persons. Is this due to married persons being wealthier on average than singles? Is it because married persons have a built in support system? Who knows the exact reason? The fact remains, married persons outlive single persons, often by significant margins. It makes one wonder if the same health benefits would apply to single persons who have good, long lasting and deep friendships?

One of my best friends is my wife, Kathy. She is my confidant, my companion, my lover, my critic, my comic relief and, most importantly, my best friend. Probably the most honest words ever written about marriage came from the pen of Dr. Joseph Sittler.

"The heart of marriage is a promise. On the face of it, it's a crazy promise: two people who have only a partial understanding of one another stand up and make this bizarre statement that they're going to cherish and care for one another for a lifetime. They say, 'I take this one and this one takes me as long as we both shall live,' not 'as long as we both shall love.' To many persons this seems like a mad and risky thing to do.

Yet I would suggest that the madness is the romance. Without risk there is no beauty, or strength, or goodness."[106]

Kathy and I were married in 1972. In those days it was very common for couples to write their own vows. Thankfully, our pastor encouraged us to create a wedding ceremony that was deeply personal and unique. I can still remember hearing my Aunt Martha weeping in the second row as we exchanged the wedding vows we had written for the occasion.

Fortunately, my brother-in-law John made an audio tape of the ceremony. We have listened to the ceremony countless times over the past 43 years and here are a few lines from the wedding:

"In companionship of one heart and one mind, two individuals come this day to make and create one home so that each, in their own way, will make the other a more complete person…"

And from the vows we wrote for each other:

"I have made my choice, I have bound myself for life. Kathy, you are to be my wife. I will no longer look to making myself happy, but I will try and make your happiness into ours. I will comfort you when you are sick, and I will be happy when you are healthy. Your sorrow and rejoicing will be mine. The riches or poverty you have, I will have also. I will not love you for what you are, but for what God has loved you for. I will love you because you are you, and I am I, and both of us are God's"[107]

The friendship of marriage has the potential of making each participant "a more complete person." When you couple that with the idea that the highest form of love is service, you have the potential of real growth and maturity.

I will never think of the word "love" without thinking of Walt. Walt, a member of a church I served, had a wife who was diagnosed with Alzheimer's disease. He kept his wife at their home for as long as he was physically able. Finally, the 24-hour care she needed was just too much. His wife was admitted to a local nursing home.

Here's where love comes in. Both Walt and his wife loved walking. While the wife's health allowed, they walked. In good weather they walked outside. In bad weather they walked at the local mall. Walt continued to take his wife walking as her mind slowly deteriorated. The walking continued for years. He walked with her even after she no longer knew her friends. He walked with her even after she couldn't recognize the stores she loved shopping at. He walked with her even after she couldn't recognize him. He walked with her without hesitation. He walked with her without embarrassment. He walked with her because he loved her.

That's what love is all about. To repeat Frederick Buechner, "love is not primarily an emotion but an act of will."

Here is how Joe Sittler describes it: "When the old guys emphasized 'for richer or for poorer, in sickness and in health' they weren't being sentimental; they meant it. A commitment like that takes guts."[108]

It is impossible to imagine human life without friends.

In your lifetime, you will have a handful that you can be totally honest with. In your lifetime you will have a handful who will be totally honest with you. In your lifetime, you will have a handful who can brave the cold winds of your loneliness. In your lifetime, you will have a handful that are wise enough to give counsel when you most need it and stay silent when you don't. In your lifetime, you will have a handful who can maintain cheerfulness in the midst of your sadness. In your lifetime, you will have a handful who will sing joyfully at your moments of gladness.

And, that handful of friends, is just about enough!

QUESTIONS FOR REFLECTION

1. Can you name a friend or friends who you could call at 4 AM in the morning?
2. Who or what do you consider to be your "storm homes"?
3. Which friends will tell you "what you need to know and not what you want to hear"?
4. Have you ever walked into the glass factory and felt like picking up a hammer? How did you handle it?
5. Have you experienced unconditional love in your life? Who, what, when and how?

6. Evaluate the good things & bad things about your closest friend. Evaluate the good things & bad things about yourself. How are they similar? How are they different?
7. If you are married, what are the ways your spouse makes you a more complete person? How do you make your spouse a more complete person?
8. List your top three friends? What are the blessings they bring to your life? Have you told them about these blessings?

Chapter 7

Chapter 7: Summary

7. ***"A ship in the harbor is safe but that is not what ships are made for."***[109]

How do we face and make the big decisions in our life? A person of faith might ask, "How do I know what God's will is for my life?" Someone who chooses to approach big decisions outside the scope of faith might ask, "How do I know whether this is the right move, to the right place and done at the right time in my life?" In this chapter I will look back on some of the big decisions my wife and I have made over the years. I believe that these moves were not random. I trust and believe that the hand of God was involved, even if I could not see that hand at the time. Finally, what chapter on journeys would be complete without a word about the ultimate and final journey of humankind?

"A ship in the harbor is safe but that is not what ships are made for."[110]

Life is a journey, but it's not a random journey.

Our life's journey is rarely a straight line. Most times, our life's journey is a terribly crooked path. Sometimes, our life's journey seems as smooth as sailing quietly through a calm bay. Other times, our life's journey is like sailing through a risk filled, raging sea. But, make no mistake about it, ships and lives are meant for journeys.

In the first 13 years of our marriage, my wife and I moved 11 times. No, the moves were not because we were running from the law. No, the moves were not because we were evicted by landlords. No, the moves were not because I worked for IBM (some punsters have said, IBM stands for "**I**'ve **B**een **M**oved"). No, looking back on these moves, I realize there was a guidance and purpose to them. Most of the time, I did not fully understood that guidance and purpose.

The biggest move in those early days was not even a move at all. It was really a kind of re-direction. I still remember going into my college adviser's office to ask for a change in my major. At the time my major was business. I decided to make a change to social sciences. Naturally, my adviser asked me my reason for wanting to change my major.

How would I explain it to her? How could I tell her that I had experienced a religious awakening so powerful that I immediately knew what my life's calling would be?

This change in direction came by virtue of an invitation to attend a dorm discussion led by Ned Hale, a regional director for Inter-Varsity Christian Fellowship. Ned, who had a theology degree from Yale, gave a presentation on Jesus Christ. By the end of that talk it was clear to me that this Jesus was as alive today as he was 2,000 years ago. Even though I had been raised in the Christian faith, it became clear to me that this living Jesus was calling me to a relationship with him and to a life of service in the world around me. I was called to respond to this Jesus and to make a difference with my life. For me, this call meant preparing to be a pastor.

So, let's get back to my college advisor. I just said to her that I decided to enter seminary after college and that a social science degree would better fit the path I was planning.

Did I really say, "The path **I** was planning"? Here's the funny thing about paths. Do we ever choose the path or does the path choose us?

Woody Allen once quipped,

"Do you know how to make God laugh?" Answer: "Tell God your plans!"[111]

Here is how Richard Halverson, former Chaplain of the United States Senate puts it, "Wherever you go, God is sending you, wherever you are, God has put you there; God has a purpose in your being there. Christ who dwells in you has something he wants to do through you, where you are. Believe this and go in His grace and love and power."[112]

This chapter is about life as a journey. As I said earlier, journeys can be straight and smooth or crooked and hazardous. Here is the plain fact. We are all on a special journey, unique to our background and gifts. While my exchange with the college advisor sounded confident and assured, you can be certain that the journey to follow that call to ministry wasn't always so confident and assured.

The 11 moves in the first 13 years of marriage is a testament to the interruptions, road blocks and delays that I experienced along the way. Sometimes the path can be just plain confusing.

Perhaps Thomas Merton put it best in this prayer:

"My Lord God: I have no idea where I am going. I do not see the road ahead. I cannot know for certain where it will end. I cannot even say that I really know myself. And, the fact that I "think" that I am following your will, does not mean I am actually doing so.

But, I believe that the desire to please you does in fact please you!! And I hope I have that desire in all that I am doing… Therefore I will trust you always, even though I may seem to be lost and might even be walking in the shadow of death. I will not fear, for you are ever with me, and you will never leave me to face my perils alone. "[113]

Abraham Lincoln put it even more bluntly, "Everyone tells me what God's will is. I wish God would tell me."[114]

I am not going to bore you with all of the 11 moves in 13 years. Frankly, many of those moves were not very interesting or difficult. After all, how hard can a move be when you can fit all your earthly possessions in a 6' by 6' U-Haul trailer?

However, I do want to begin with the first detour along the way. Remember how I told my college advisor that I was changing majors in preparation to enter seminary. What changed that plan?

Kathy and I were married at the end of the first semester of my senior year in college. We rented a trailer just outside of my college town and set up our first "home." It's amazing how you can look back on humble beginnings with nostalgia and think, those were the "good ol days."

I remember that last semester of college as a happy and peaceful time.

We lived in a two-bedroom trailer. I carried a lunch of tuna fish sandwiches in my book bag. We grilled hamburgers on a 10 inch square Hibachi grill. Our income consisted of money Kathy earned as a secretary and the occasional monetary gift from home. This, pretty much, describes our simple and joyful life.

I still have an old photograph of that first "happy home." The picture is my 1966 Ford Mustang parked in front of the trailer. The car is covered with a foot of Wisconsin snow.

That photo reminds me of the night I almost burned that trailer to the ground. In the dead of winter, I tried barbequing on our enclosed wooden porch using our Hibachi grill. I succeeded in filling the trailer full of smoke each time I opened the door to check on the grill. Despite the death defying cooking method, those burgers were delicious.

But I digress. What caused that first detour on the path to seminary? Was it confusion, hunger or greed? Actually it was none of the above. The simple fact was, at the end of four years of college, I just could not face another four years of schooling. I had to get out and make a living in the "real" world.

So, I began to look for a job.

I had added a major in secondary education to my social science degree. I was even offered a job teaching history where I had completed my student teaching. But, I knew that teaching was not really my passion, so I began to search for other options.

Here's where you will begin to hear me repeat the theme from this chapter's title, "A ship in the harbor is safe but that's not what ships are made for." You see, when presented with the "safe" option over the more risky option, we somehow always chose the riskier one. We seemed to always leave the "safe" harbor.

In 1973 the United States was entering into one of the many economic downturns in its history. I can prove it. Just do an internet search. Type the words "recession of 1973 – 1975." You will read about the economic uncertainty of those days.

So, what did I do? Did I take the safe and more secure choice of a teaching position? No. Turning down that "safe" teaching job may have been the first "risky" decision Kathy and I made.

As I said earlier, teaching was not my passion. Instead of taking the teaching job, I decided to take a sales job with a major copier company.

Getting the job was no easy task considering the recession of 1973, but I was persistent. I can remember going through a series of five interviews before I was offered the job as a sales trainee for the copier company. One of those interviews is described earlier in Chapter 4. I am convinced that I got the sales job by answering one particular question with honesty and integrity. You'll have to turn back to Chapter 4 for that story.

Taking the sales job was riskier than taking the teaching job, but ships are meant to sail out of harbors and that is exactly what Kathy and I did. I took the sales job and bought my first two business suits at Robert Hall Department Store. As I recall, the suits were two for $99 in 1973. Kathy and I then moved to our first rental house. It was a small, cozy, two-bedroom rental located on Hillside Drive in Franklin Grove, Illinois.

What a dramatic turnaround from the two-bedroom trailer! We were now living in a small, two-bedroom house with a one car garage. It had TWO yards, a front yard and a back yard! The back yard even had a patch for a garden and some wild asparagus growing along the fence line. It was right on the edge of town looking out over the rich farmland of north central Illinois.

I covered a two county sales territory and Kathy got a job as a secretary for the University of Illinois Agricultural Extension Office. During this same time, Kathy finished her bachelor's degree in business education at Northern Illinois University. NIU was a one hour commute from our Franklin Grove home.

The job in sales would be the absolute best training for the journeys that were to come, but I get ahead of myself.

We were living the American Dream. We bought our first used boat. We invested in our first piece of rental real estate. We bought our first new cars. With some sweat equity, we even moved into our first home (thanks to a modern financial instrument called a mortgage). Did you know mortgage is a French term literally meaning "death contract?"

Our first "owned" house was a small, three-bedroom ranch on a wooded lot just outside of Dixon, Illinois. The house was a "National Home". These homes were built in factories, taken apart and then shipped to the customer on a truck. The one exceptional feature in our new home was the stone fireplace built by my father, the stone mason.

To my wife and I the first home we owned was a mansion. It was a mansion with less than 1,500 square feet, but who cares. Even the name of the subdivision declared prestige. We had built our modest, three-bedroom home, on a wooded lot in "Chateau Woods." Unfortunately, we lived in that house for less than eight months.

Did I remember to tell you that when faced with the safe and easy path or the hard and challenging one...

We chose the hard, challenging path again.

Remember the discussion with my college advisor? Remember the confident and assured manner of describing my plans to enter seminary? That was in 1970. It was now 1976, but that call still had a hold on me. You see, "there is a big difference between an affluent life and an abundant life."[115] There was nothing essentially wrong with where we were, what we were doing, and the things we had accomplished. It just seemed like I needed to fulfill a bigger purpose with my life.

Speaking of purpose, I especially like the way Pastor Rick Warren puts it. He says, "Without a purpose, life is motion without meaning, activity without direction and events without reason. Never confuse activity with productivity."[116]

Without question, this move would be one of the hardest ones we would ever make. We had come to enjoy our new home. I had a secure and comfortable job. To top that off, Kathy had been offered a teaching job at Dixon High School where she had done her student teaching. That teaching job would be only 10 minutes from our new home. But, as I said in Chapter 1:

> ...you want to spend that time doing something
> you enjoy. More to the point, you want to spend
> that time doing what you feel "called" to do.
> The word "vocation: comes from the Latin word

"vocare", to call. Work then is not just a pursuit to put bread on the table. No, work is a God given opportunity to use our time and abilities not only for our own good but also for the good of others. To find a fit between what your gifts are and a job that needs to be done can make work a pleasure instead of a burden, a blessing instead of a curse.

Remember how I described taking the riskier path three years earlier. I took the sales job over the teaching job? Well, here we go again.

It turns out, that at the same time Kathy was offered the Dixon teaching job, she also saw a teaching opening at the Jo Daviess-Carrol Area Vocational Center in Elizabeth, Illinois (located less than 60 miles from Wartburg Seminary in Dubuque, Iowa). Could this be God's way of providing a stepping stone to that seminary path that had chosen me many years earlier? I encouraged Kathy to take the interview, and with fear and trepidation she agreed. The interview went very well. She was immediately offered the job at the vocational center. As I recall, Kathy was asked to make her decision in a short period of time.

What would it mean taking the "riskier" position in Elizabeth, Illinois? It was certainly too far a distance to commute from our present home. It would mean selling our first "dream home" after living in it less than eight months. It would mean making another move to a new community.

It would also open the door to the path of entering seminary. Where and how was God leading us and what steps would we be asked to take? Looking back, I can see those steps much more clearly now than I did then.

STEP ONE was accepting or rejecting the offer to take the teaching position which was out of town in Elizabeth, Illinois.

I remember agonizing over the decision before, during and after the interview. Could this be the door that was opening toward seminary and pastoral ministry? Kathy had always known of my desire to follow this path, but it was going to require big sacrifices. Could I ask those sacrifices of her? Could I ask those sacrifices of myself? After agonizing about the decision and prayerful discernment, we came to the decision that Kathy would take the out of town teaching job. Taking the teaching job would be the first step toward moving on to seminary.

STEP TWO was to apply to Wartburg Theological Seminary in Dubuque, Iowa.

Application and acceptance to seminary is no certainty. Fortunately, I had pastors and a number of great folks at my home church who gave me good references. In addition, my decision to change careers had the support of my wife and my family. I received acceptance to seminary in the summer of 1976. Once accepted into seminary it was on to step three.

STEP THREE was to put our house up for sale.

Obviously, we hated to sell the new home we had worked so hard to build. What if the house didn't sell? Step three was a big financial sacrifice to face. The first thing we did was put up a "For Sale by Owner" sign in our front yard.

Two or three days after the sign went up I was making a transaction at our local Savings and Loan. One of the personal bankers came up to me and asked if we were really selling our new home. I said yes and explained my plans for moving away to begin my seminary education. She asked if she and her husband could make an appointment to come and see our house.

They looked at our house, made us an offer and we sold it to them in the next week. The closing went quickly because the new owner worked for the same Savings and Loan who had financed the home less than six months earlier.

STEP FOUR was to find a new home to live in that was within commuting distance to Kathy's teaching job and the seminary in Dubuque.

My in laws had just recently built a summer home near Apple Canyon Lake, Illinois. The home had plumbing and electrical but was so new that it did not even have carpet on the floor. Kathy and I asked her parents if we could rent the home during the four years that I would be attending seminary. They were happy to have the home occupied, especially in the winter months.

Now we would have a place to live within commuting distance of seminary and Kathy's job. My in laws would also have caretakers for their new summer home.

STEP FIVE was to resign from my sales position.

Fred, the District Sales Manager, was shocked when I sat down in his office to explain that I was resigning to attend seminary in the fall. I can still remember the look on his face and his struggle to understand my decision. Then, in his confusion on how to respond, he blurted out this amazing question.

"Well Jack, is it a matter of money? If it's a matter of money, I can see what can be done about getting you a promotion and a raise."

Not to brag, but in the last year I had already received a promotion to "Senior Sales Representative." The promotion had come with a nice raise. I also had received multiple "salesman of the month" awards and even been named "salesman of the quarter" for the last quarter of 1975. To be honest, I made a comfortable living. This seminary decision was clearly not about money.

How could I explain to Fred that my decision was not about money but about "call?" I was both challenged and rewarded by my job. I was enjoying the financial freedom of earning a generous salary and commissions. Despite all this, I knew there was another path I was being called to follow.

Since my high school days I had been told by members of my church that I would make a good pastor. In Lutheran terms, we refer to those encouragements as an "outward call." Now that "outward call" would be matched with the "inward call" to leave the sales vocation and to prepare for pastoral ministry.

Fred, in confusion, could only offer me more money. Harry, my first sales manager, got it. At my parting luncheon, Harry presented me with an engraved "Cross" pen and pencil set. The set had been special ordered with a gold cross prominently affixed. Harry, who was a devout Catholic, got it. He knew that I now would be using skills and experiences learned through sales in a "higher" calling.

STEP SIX, our sixth move in our four-year-old marriage was in the summer of 1976.

The six steps involved in this major move seem smooth and orderly, but nothing could be further from the truth. They only seem that way AFTER the events occurred. It almost seemed as if God was placing stepping stones before us. The stones were placed there one at a time. Step out here and wait. Step out here and wait. There were doubts at every step, but assurance and more clarity at the end. What a powerful lesson to prepare us for future moves we would have to consider on our journey.

"A ship in the harbor is safe...

Have I mentioned that when presented with the "safe" option over the more risky option, we somehow always chose the riskier one?

The next major decision we would face would be just after graduation from seminary. Each seminarian is assigned to a geographical territory. My assigned geographical synod was northern Wisconsin. Now, do you remember the pattern of taking the risky path versus the safe one?

A few months before my graduation from seminary, the rural church Kathy and I had attended needed a new pastor. My wife and I had enjoyed that church. We made many new friends there. My son had been baptized there in August of 1978, just before we left on a year-long internship assignment near Washington D.C.

Pursuing a call to this familiar congregation would certainly be the "safe" option. We could continue to be near our families. We could maintain our friendships with the church community we had come to know.

…"but that's not what ships are made for."

We took the riskier path again. We interviewed and received our first call to a two-point church. One of the churches was in Chippewa Falls, Wisconsin and the other church was outside of Cadott, Wisconsin. It took more than a 6' by 6' U-Haul trailer this time. In the summer of 1980, Kathy, baby Nathan and I moved to a parsonage just outside of Chippewa Falls, Wisconsin.

Why does everyone seem to remember their first salaries? It is probably because that is the first amount of money that you had to find a way to actually survive on. Maybe it is because it looks so small compared to what is required to live on years later.

I can still remember my first salary as a called pastor. It was $12,500 plus a parsonage and utilities. This was a little higher than the salary guidelines of $11,800 for new seminarians. I guess the congregation figured I was worth it since, unlike other new seminary graduates, I had three extra years of life and business experience.

What is even more amazing is what the retired, interim pastor told me after I arrived. Pastor Ernst said that my starting salary was higher than the salary he was making in his last full year of ministry.

Keep in mind that his ending salary was what he was earning after serving churches for over 30 years! Now, to be blunt, I am convinced that Pastor Ernst was 50% responsible for that. I can imagine he had made many "noble sacrifices" in those 30 years. He may have even turned down a few proposed raises in those years. He had probably rationalized those noble sacrifices by saying, "Times are hard. They just can't afford it right now." In my humble opinion, he had done neither himself nor his churches a service in the process. The silent thief of inflation eats away at purchasing power, especially to those who stay at the same salary.

If I was looking for a vocation where I could put Chapter 1 of this book into practice, this was the vocation to have. Wow, this book, <u>Just Plain Sense</u>, is really starting to fit together. You will now have to turn back to Chapter 1 to be reminded of what it is that I had to put into practice.

The Chippewa Falls area is where I began applying what I had learned in seminary classes, clinical pastoral education and internship. Chippewa Falls is a beautiful area of lakes, forests, farmland and small communities. It is home to honest, hardworking folks. My daughter Terra was born there in 1981.

My son Nathan and daughter Terra had their own miniature sledding hill and miniature playground nestled in the woods behind our parsonage. It was a wonderful place to live and serve.

Have I mentioned that when presented with the "safe" option over the more risky option, we somehow always chose the riskier one? I sense the description of another move is coming here.

It is a fairly common thing for new pastors, especially ones in smaller congregations, to get a telephone call from a bigger, more prosperous church. This is especially true if the pastor is reasonably liked and the church or churches they are serving are growing in numbers and faithfulness. The word has a way of getting out because a denominational network has lots of informal grapevines.

After I had served in my first call for three years I received two such telephone calls. I responded to the first telephone call by saying that I was basically happy where I was currently serving. However, I told the pastor on that first telephone call that I was honored that my name came up for consideration. In truth, I basically said, "Thanks --but no thanks."

The second telephone call I took much more seriously. It was from a very large and prestigious church in a nearby college town. The senior pastor's name was even Jack. What kind of nickname would I have to be given if I took this call? It was a call with a higher salary, better housing and a town with a shopping mall to boot!

Here is where the theme of "risky" paths continues. Also, here is where the pieces of this book and my call to be a mission developer begin to fit together. I will have to borrow again from Chapter 1 of <u>Just Plain Sense</u> to fit the pieces together.

Never work for money or power.

> *I will never forget a day in 1984 when I met Susan Thompson, mission director for the Division of Service and Mission in America. She had just given an address to a church convention. It was about the need for pastor developers to plant new churches. Un-churched people need to hear the gospel message. It was a call to be a missionary, but not to a foreign land. It was a call to reach out with the gospel right here at home.*

I went up to Susan Thompson after that address and introduced myself with these words, "Hi, my name is Jack Ottoson and my internship pastor once told me that I should consider being a mission developer."

Susan told me later, that after speaking with me for 10 minutes she knew I would make a good mission developer. A true vocation seeks you, not the other way around.

There are many paths that an ordained pastor can take. You can serve in small towns, big cities, old churches, new churches, traumatized churches, family churches or ethnic churches. You can enter teaching, chaplaincy work or administration.

The question still remains for you and me: "What will I work for?" "How can I best match my gifts and passions in earning a living?" "What is my true call in life?" I think Frederick Buechner has it exactly right when he says, "The place God calls you to, is the place where your deepest gladness and the world's deepest hunger meet."[17]

As I remember it, the phone call from the "large and prestigious church" and the initial meeting with Susan Thompson, the Mission Director, happened around the same time.

Here is where the "risky" versus the "safe" path show up again.

The safe path was before me. I could pursue what some would consider the safer, larger, more prestigious call. Or, I could pursue the riskier call offered in the form of serving as a mission developer.

Here is where another piece of my life and this book come into focus. Why the choice of the risky sales job over the safe teaching job? Why the 3 year delay in going to seminary? Could it be that those years in the sales profession had prepared me, unknowingly, for the next 30 years of pastoral ministry?

As you recall, in 1973 I had taken the riskier path of sales over the safer path of teaching. Looking back on my time in sales I am amazed at how well those years prepared me to eventually become a mission developer. Here are a few of the skills and traits that the sales vocation and the mission development vocation have in common.

SELF STARTER: Both vocations provide special training for the task at hand, but being a self-starter is essential in both sales and mission development. My parent's generation would describe this trait as being a "go-getter." I suppose that means being a person who takes initiative and can succeed with minimal supervision. He or she is more a doer than a thinker.

PERSONABLE: It is said, "You never get a second chance to make a first impression." If you think about it, this is especially true in sales and mission development. Both vocations depend a great deal on making good first impressions whether it is to a potential customer or to a potential church member. In the initial stage of a new church, the pastor/developer is the first witness and face of the new church. There is no building, no pipe organ, no choir, and no youth program. There is basically a new pastor, going door to door, house to house. His or her call involves introducing and inviting unchurched people in the community to this new worshipping community.

FLEXIBLE: Life is not just about good days and bad days. Life is about how we handle good days and bad days. There will indeed be both. When it comes right down to it, "success" in ministry has more to do with AV (Adversity Quotient) than IQ (Intelligence Quotient) or EQ (Emotional Quotient). AV will serve you much better than IQ or EQ when money runs short, the council president resigns or the choir sings off tune. Business consultant, Paul Stotlz, puts it this way. "People can be divided into three categories, climbers seeking challenge, quitters fleeing from challenge and the broad, fleshy middle, called campers. These folks just want to know what's for lunch."[118]

PERSISTENCE AND THE ABILITY TO TAKE REJECTION: In sales, we called them "cold calls." In mission development, they are called door to door "evangelism." Whether the message is about the latest product or the greatest story ever told, some people just aren't interested. It boils down to rejection. Someone either doesn't want what you have to offer or they already have a church home. You must be able to handle rejection. It happened to Moses, it happened to the prophets and it happened to Jesus. Guess what? It is bound to happen to mission developers.

Here are some humbling statistics. While 10% of people may come to a church drawn by the pastor, 80% will be drawn by an invitation of a neighbor or friend. Out of 1,000 contacts made, only a handful of folks might actually join the new congregation.

Case in point: I will never forget the pleasant visit I had with Marv and Rose. They were genuinely welcoming and interested in the new church. Can you guess how long it was before they made their first visit to our church in Kenosha? Their first visit to our new church was two years after knocking on their door! Did I mention persistence?

So, we've come to move number 10 in those first 13 years of marriage. This move would be from Chippewa Falls to Kenosha, Wisconsin. I was being called by the national church to be a "pastor/developer." In common terms, that is a domestic missionary.

As I explained above, the call to mission development began with the encouragement of my internship pastor. It continued with the skills developed in sales. Now, after interviewing with Mission Director, Susan Thompson, the call to be a pastor/developer would be issued. It arrived from the Division of Service and Mission of our national church body.

Talk about risk, this was a call to a local church that didn't even exist! Well actually, that might be exaggerating a little bit, but not by much. The first "informational" meeting for the new church was held at the home of Karen & Jim on November

14, 1984. There were seven people at that meeting. That's not exactly the biblical number of 12, but it was a start.

I have to say that those days were some of the most challenging and exciting days in my 30 years of ministry. Every pastor I have spoken to who has "planted" a new church says that being a pastor/developer was the most fulfilling time of their ministry. I couldn't agree with them more! These times were not easy, but they were very exciting.

I can remember speaking with Mission Director, Susan Thompson, in the first months of the new church start. I jokingly said, "Susan, this is about the most fun you can have without going to jail!"

But wait just a minute. Have I deceived you? Have I deceived myself? Have I led you to believe that I have always taken the hard and risky path when actually I haven't? Truth be told, the path was risky but not as hard as you might think.

I may not have always taken the safe path but at least I had taken the most passionate one. Confucius said, "Choose a job you love and you will never have to work another day in your life."[119] While this might be overstating it a bit, I had truly found my passion.

For me, mission development was, as Frederick Buechner says, "the place where my deepest gladness and the world's deepest hunger met." It is a "thank God it's Monday" experience.

"A career is not the same as a vocation. Nearly every modern person is required to forge some kind of career, but a vocation involves a calling or summoning. We may choose a career, but a vocation chooses us."[120] In this case, mission development had chosen me.

Move 10 from Chippewa Falls to Kenosha was much more difficult and complicated than the previous moves. Kathy and I now had lots more "stuff." Much more "stuff" than we could ever fit in a 6' by 6' U-Haul. We also had a 6-year-old son and a 3-year-old daughter joining us on our move. The blessing for them and us is that Kenosha was three hours closer to their two sets of grandparents.

We initially settled into a tiny Cape Cod home in Kenosha. The rental house was a stone's throw from Carthage College and located on a beautiful bluff overlooking Lake Michigan. Since this chapter pieces together other parts of this book, this is where the "moving in" story from Chapter 5 fits.

> *When my son was 6 and my daughter was 3, we made a major relocation. We moved into a quaint but small two-story house. Fortunately for us we didn't own lots of furniture, but my son did sleep in a rather large bunk bed. It was hand made by his grandpa.*
>
> *Unfortunately, the bunk bed was too tall to assemble in his tiny upstairs bedroom. The sloped ceiling would mean that only the bottom bunk*

could be used to sleep in because the top bunk was right up against the ceiling. Trying to create the most positive construction on the problem we explained it this way to our son. We said, if he had friends over, rather than sleep on the upper bulk we could place the mattresses on the bedroom floor and they could sleep like "china men." (Forgive us here. My wife and I know all Chinese people do not sleep on the floor! We were just trying to make lemonade out of lemons.)

When my 3-year-old daughter heard about this arrangement she began crying inconsolably. After she calmed down enough to be understood through her sobbing, she declared with crocodile tears in her eyes, "but I want to sleep like a china man too!"… We had made lemonade out of lemons, and our 3-year-old daughter wanted a taste of that lemonade.

I recall that we did, in fact, allow our daughter to move her mattress to the floor to try sleeping like a China man. However, she soon tired of this arrangement and we moved the mattress back onto her bed frame.

So, where is move number 11? We are finally there.

Move number 11 was in 1985 and not nearly as dramatic as the previous ones. A generous church member gave a residential lot to the new mission church and a brand new parsonage was built on that gift of land. That move was like returning back to 1976 when we had built and moved into our first new home. Even though we didn't own this home, at least we were able to make the choices of the interior colors and carpet. My son and daughter even got to pick the color of their bedrooms. And what about that big bunk bed? My son's new room was big enough to fit that bunk bed with room to spare.

The new mission church prospered in the years from 1985 through 1996. Our initial worship location was the Bullen Junior High School auditorium.

I can still remember a slide photo we would show on road trips to older, more established congregations. One slide showed our tiny Renault Alliance car. Standing in front of the car were my wife, my son, my daughter and me. A sandwich board sign is displayed next to us. The large print reads...

LORD of LIFE LUTHERAN CHURCH
Meeting at Bullen Jr. High School
Sunday at 9:00 A.M.

Everyone in the picture is carrying something. The standard joke I would make is, "If you are a pastor/developer with children, the kids better be big enough to carry something." Actually that is really the truth. The early days of church development are days of carrying and borrowing. You borrow a place to have worship. You borrow a place to hold meetings. You borrow a place to have choir practice, bible studies, and dinners. One result of those "borrowings" is a deep sense of community developed among the first members.

In May of 1991, after worshipping at Bullen Junior High for over six years, we dedicated our new church building. What a day of celebration that was!

Honored guests were there. The contractor handed over the keys to the building. The local newspaper was there. We had food and special music. It was a spectacular day of celebration and pride in the new building we had built.

Have I mentioned that when presented with the "safe" option over the more risky option, we somehow always chose the riskier one?

I said earlier that my wife and I moved 11 times in our first 13 years of marriage. So, the moves are not over at number 11.

Seven interested people became the core of Lord of Life Lutheran Church in 1985. That group grew to over 450 by 1996. The church had built a new building, added a second worship service and was faithfully serving the community in multiple ways.

In the early days, 1986 to be exact, Lord of Life had purchased four acres of land on a busy highway. The first thing we did was plant evergreen trees around the perimeter of our new land. Since there was not yet a public water line or a well to draw water from, church members lovingly hand carried water to those seedling trees. A family would adopt a row of trees. They would see to it that those thirsty seedling were cared for. What a fitting image of the body of Christ. Jesus said it best, "Truly, I say to you, as you did it to one of the least of these..."[121]

Oh, sorry. That parable is about caring for people in need, not trees. Well, you get my point. We learned to live out the meaning of service through watering each fragile seedling. It would be great training for other ministries of service, like feeding the hungry and homeless.

Here comes risky move--number 12.

Remember when I said, "Every pastor I have spoken to who has 'planted' a new church says that being a pastor/developer was the most fulfilling time of their ministry"? I forgot to tell you what they usually said next. It went something like, "I will never do THAT again!"

In spring of 1996, I did THAT again. Kathy, Nathan and I took a spring break trip to Florida. Nathan was looking at attending Florida Atlantic University in Boca Raton, Florida. At the same time, Kathy and I were interviewing with Ron Ryckman, the Mission Director from Florida. A month earlier, I had spoken to Ron about my interest in "doing THAT again." The THAT was developing a new congregation.

So, you might think the risky move was "doing THAT again." Actually it's not that simple. Have I mentioned that when presented with the safe option over the more risky option, we somehow always chose the riskier one?

Less than one month prior to flying down to Florida to consider the new mission start, I received a phone call from my bishop, Peter Rogness. Bishop Rogness wanted to meet for lunch. Now, when your bishop wants to have lunch with you there are usually two things that it can mean.

1. He/she is going to ask you to do something. OR
2. He/she is going to reveal what kind of dog house you are in. Then you have to figure out how to get out of that dog house.

I was sort of relieved that it was #1 and not #2. I say "sort of" because Peter was asking me to consider taking a new call in a neighboring Wisconsin community. The original pastor/developer was leaving a congregation which had been under development for just a few years. The bishop was asking me to continue where the mission developer had left off. It would mean leading a congregation from the first stage of growth in and through a building stage and beyond.

There were some decidedly positive things about the request. It certainly wouldn't be as huge a move as going to Florida. My wife might be able to commute to her present job if we moved to the Wisconsin community. My children could stay in Wisconsin where they had been raised. The move to the new Wisconsin community would most certainly be a challenge, but not as big a challenge as moving to Florida. What kind of answer would I give to him?

Bishop Rogness already knew I enjoyed mission development. He also knew that I was open to "doing THAT again." He also knew I was going to Florida to talk with the mission director there. (In our church system, it is required protocol to inform one's bishop about a desire to move to another geographical area.)

I asked Bishop Peter for time to complete my Florida visit. After that visit I would make my decision about the call in Wisconsin. He said, "fair enough".

"A ship in the harbor is safe...

So, you see the decision was really between the safety of staying in the harbor or sailing off to one or the other of the new calls.

I came back from the spring trip to Daytona Beach, Florida feeling that this was where I was being called to next.

Without question, move number 12 was the most difficult move of them all. Why?

Now my decision would not just involve lugging furniture and "stuff" around the country. Now my decision would dramatically affect the three people I loved the most. Kathy would have to leave friends and a fulfilling, lucrative job at the technical college. Nathan would have to leave local friends to attend college in the "foreign" land of Boca Raton, Florida. Terra would have to leave her friends in Kenosha and join the many other vagabond youth who move to Florida every year.

On Sunday, June 16, 1996, here is what was on the church sign at Lord of Life Lutheran Church in Kenosha, Wisconsin.

"A ship in the harbor is safe but that is not what ships are made for."

On Saturday, June 22, 1996, the Kenosha News had an article about me and move number 12. The article was very complimentary. Here is a portion of that article.

> The sign outside Lord of Life Lutheran Church last Sunday told passersby:
>
> "A ship in the harbor is safe but that is not what ships are made for."
>
> And while the congregation inside the beautiful church at Hwy 31 and Washington Road, would likely have agreed philosophically, their church is the harbor and their much loved minister the ship, so philosophy gave way to tears…
>
> But why him? Why not stay here and bask in the love of the many people who have come to know him… "One time I was at a church convention and I went up to the mission director for the state," he began, leading up to his answer. "I told her that my supervising pastor in seminary told me I would be a good pastor to develop new churches. The mission director told me later that she knew, by talking

to me only five minutes, that developing churches was my calling in life."[122]

About a month before Kathy, Nathan, Terra and I left on the next grand journey to Daytona Beach, Florida, I separated my shoulder playing racquetball. I walked around with my right arm immobilized in a sling.

For me, it is the primary image of move number 12. To me, leaving behind a congregation that I had built, nurtured, cajoled, loved and served would be like losing my right arm. There will always be a part of me left behind in those 12 years of ministry at Lord of Life Lutheran Church. I think my wife and children have some of those same feelings about leaving Wisconsin.

In Chapter 5, I quote Fr. Mike Mack, my Clinical Pastoral Education supervisor.

"Growth=Change"
"Change=Loss of Old"
"Loss=Grief"
"Grief=Pain"
"Growth=Pain"[123]

Those words ring true as I think back to July of 1996.

The Bible is filled with stories about journeys of faith. Think of the Bible characters who took those amazing journeys. There is Abraham, Isaac, Jacob, Joseph, Moses, Joshua, David, Jeremiah, Esther, Jesus and Paul...just to name a few. Those pilgrims of the faith lived out the classic dialectic between continuity and change. Our own journeys of faith are instructed and encouraged by those biblical pilgrims and their stories. Those pilgrims understood life as a journey where choosing faithfulness to the call of God often meant risk and change.

I was indeed, "doing it again" with the crazy assurance that God was supporting and even blessing the move. The Spirit of God had preceded me to this new "foreign land." In my crazy optimism I told people, "The church is already there. My only job is to gather the people of this new, unorganized congregation into a living, breathing, worshipping congregation." Sounds easy doesn't it?

The first "informational" meeting for Daytona Beach's new church was held in our living room at 113 Green wing Teal Court. As I recall, there were around 17 people at that meeting. It was actually an improvement over the seven at the first "informational" meeting for the Kenosha mission. I was now a little older and presumably a little wiser. I had the experience of organizing the congregation in Kenosha. I mean, how hard could this be?

I would come to realize that this would be a bigger challenge than my first mission congregation. Florida was not "Lutheran" country like Wisconsin was. This was 1996 not 1984. The demographics, the price of Florida land (six acres of Florida land was $415,000, compared to four acres of Wisconsin land at $31,000) and the attitudes of the unchurched or the formerly churched would be factors making the Florida new church development much harder than Wisconsin. Starting with 17 people in Daytona Beach is better than starting with seven people in Kenosha, but the Florida mission work would be harder at every juncture.

An important first task in any new church start up is finding a place to worship. It was no different in Daytona Beach. Soon after arriving in Daytona Beach, I made a visit to the campus of Embry Riddle University. I introduced myself to the chapel coordinator Mary Ellen and Robert, the Dean of Student Affairs. By coincidence or divine design, it so happened that the university's volunteer Protestant chaplain had just retired. Mary Ellen's last question before I left her office was, "Our volunteer chaplain has just retired and spends summers two states away. Would you be available to help in pastoral emergencies?"

I assured her that she could call on me if a need arose.

Weeks later I received a call from Mary Ellen. A professor had died suddenly and tragically. Would I help? I said "yes, of course." That was the first of hundreds of services I would hold at the Embry Riddle University Chapel between 1996 and 2007.

You see, in the fall of 1996, our new congregation signed an agreement to lease chapel space from Embry Riddle University. I was also named as the new volunteer Protestant chaplain. Was it coincidence or divine design? I choose to call it a marriage made in heaven. It was good for Embry

Riddle and good for the new mission church, Hope Lutheran. Why? Simply put, the school had a volunteer chaplain and the church had a place to worship.

Is life's journey filled with coincidences, luck or divine design? That is a question that has been debated since the beginning of human consciousness. The following story won't solve the dilemma, but it's a good story none the less.

In the first few months of mission development in Daytona Beach, an office bill of $400.70 came due. Support funds had not yet arrived from our denomination's headquarters. I had no idea how to pay the $400.70 bill. Within days of receiving the bill for $400.07 I received a generous donation from a person who was excited about a new Lutheran church being started in Daytona Beach. The check was for $400!!

I wrote in the next newsletter…The gift of $400 was as if God was telling me, "Here is what you need. If you don't have the faith to come up with 70 cents, then you are in the wrong business!"

Bob and Audrey, were on the newsletter mailing list at the time. They also sent a generous contribution to the new church. It was not an even dollar amount. It had 70 cents after the dollar amount. In their kind note were these words,

"Guess what the $.70 on the check is for? Read your newsletter. We wish you the best, Jack. God will guide and throw in a little 'luck' as well."[124]

Maybe it is not theologically sound, but "the harder you work the luckier you get."[125]

After the 2007 celebration and dedication of the new church building for Hope Lutheran Church of Daytona Beach, I decided to create a journal of the trials we went through along the way. I titled it "Hurdles & Roadblocks." What an eye opener!

What was the final number of hurdles and roadblocks? I came up with no less than 70. There is a saying that goes, "Know that if God sends you down rocky paths, God will also provide you with strong shoes." In those nine years, we dealt with no less than 30 professionals and agencies. We had delays caused by bureaucracies, hurricanes, construction material shortages, price hikes and lack of money.

So, how was the building of the new church accomplished? Was it by coincidence, luck, hard work or divine design? Maybe it was all four, but I am convinced that God's hand was in it from the beginning.

The prophet says, "For I know the plans I have for you, says the Lord, plans for welfare and not for evil, to give you a future and a hope."[126] The irony here is that Jeremiah, of all the prophets, was a prophet most resistant to answering the call he was "made for."

Sometimes the journey we follow seems like it is uphill all the way. Sometimes we begin to doubt whether we are cut out for a job, a task or a post. We would just as soon return to the safe harbor we sailed out of.

The hard challenges tempt us to give up and return to the quiet and familiar. Yet, when we believe there is a purpose to our journey, we seem to have an inner source of strength and purpose that keeps us moving forward. Despite all the storms and challenges, we adjust our sails and move on.

"A ship in the harbor is safe but that is not what ships are made for."

On January 1, 2009, I sailed the ship in a new direction. I sailed into retirement. I was 57 and a half at the time. Now, realistically, I probably look close to my age so many people said, "You are too young to retire." I honestly didn't know how to respond to that, except to say, "Thanks that must mean I look younger than I feel."

I suppose the simplest answer to why I sailed into retirement is that I could. I had planned well for eventual retirement. I was fortunate to have a wife who had a good job and was able to include me on her health care plan. I had reached a place in my calling where I felt I had accomplished significant milestones. In my calling as a mission pastor, I had guided the development and building of two churches. But in truth, this decision was more complicated than simply saying, I could.

Remember the prayer group I described in Chapter 6? In the year preceding retirement I asked the prayer group to hold me accountable for journaling my work life.

In that work life journal I was to simply write down three things.

1. Things I will miss about my life at work.
2. Things I will not miss about my life at work.
3. Things I will look forward to in retirement.

I hind sight, it was one of the best preparations I ever made for retirement. It was better than the books on retirement which I had read, the retirement inventories I had filled out or any pre-retirement seminar I ever attended.

The work life journal prepared me to say "yes" and "no" to requests after I retired. Simply put, why would you say "no" to something you anticipated missing in retirement? Vice versa, why would you say "yes" to something you would not miss?

I would be kidding you and myself if I said that health concerns or fear of dying too early didn't enter my thinking on retirement. After all, everyone looks forward to enjoying the freedom of retirement.

Here's a simple fact. I was privileged to have a calling that reminded me often of the frailty, shortness and uncertainty of life. I had two racquetball partners who died much too early--one died at age 52, the other at age 64. I was determined to retire while I still had the energy to enjoy travel, fishing, writing and volunteering.

In 2009 here is what I said to Bob, the assistant to our bishop, "Bob, there are two mistakes you can make in retirement.

One is to retire too early, the other is to retire too late. The problem is, if you retire too late, you can't go back and make the mistake of retiring too early. So, I want to make the mistake of retiring too early, first."

I've never regretted "retiring too early" as it was the right time for me.

Often the first thing people wonder about when a friend or family member retires early is their health. Do they have a condition that forced them to retire?

While health concerns wasn't my primary concern, it still was a contributing factor in my retirement. In December of 2000 I went to my family physician with complaints of joint pain, stiffness and general tiredness. What was baffling was the fact that most of the pain was in my left elbow. The truth was, I was experiencing pain in many other joints.

Now, I have played racquetball for thirty years so I am used to pain, but this pain was in my left elbow and I play the sport right handed. Luckily my doctor knew the right blood tests to order. The rheumatoid factor and "sed rate" on the blood test came back positive. That is usually an indication of rheumatoid arthritis (RA). I was both relieved and scared when I heard the diagnosis.

After receiving the diagnosis, I read lots of material about rheumatoid arthritis, but the best description of the condition came from the actress Kathleen Turner.

Kathleen Turner says, "I went to a podiatrist...he told me, essentially to buy bigger shoes...I started to be unable to turn my head, a doctor took an X-ray...no recommendation. Then it was my left elbow, the sports medicine doctor suggested exploratory surgery. Finally I went to my general practitioner. I started crying and said, 'I need help. I think I am dying...I later learned that rheumatoid arthritis is not necessarily life threatening, but it is lifestyle threatening."[127]

When I read those words from the interview with Kathleen Turner I was astounded. I could have written those same words. Here was a person, about my age, who had a medical condition almost identical to mine. The only things I would add to Kathleen Turner's list are lethargy and depression.

In my case I was fortunate to have an early diagnosis. I wasn't going crazy and I wasn't dying, but I did have a chronic disease. As a matter of fact, as another rheumatoid arthritis patient humorously puts it, "I have rheumatoid arthritis; my doctor told me it is all about attitude. You are not dying OF this disease, you are living WITH this disease. Until it kills you... then you will be dead FROM the disease."[128]

After 15 years of being in clinical trials and trying different medications I can happily report that I've been in steady remission. As a matter of fact, the last time I saw the rheumatologist was many years ago. Rheumatoid arthritis can be a sneaky culprit which wears many masks.

At the time of this writing, I have now enjoyed seven years of retirement. These years have been both rich and full. I enjoy reasonably good health, a positive attitude and a wide range of interests. I look forward to many more years of good retirement.

A ship in the harbor is safe but that is not what ships are made for.

What chapter about journeys would be complete without a word about the ultimate and final journey of humankind, the journey into death?

I had a rather melancholy conversation with my older sister. We were talking about the fact that we both have completed the main task of parenthood. We have raised our children to be responsible adults. Both of us, in our own way, were asking the question, "Is our parenting role over?" Thankfully, my children still ask for advice, but the conversations are adult ones now. The advice is more conversational than directive.

After the conversation with my sister it occurred to me that, as parents, we still have the most important lesson to pass on to them. I am thinking about the lessons we pass on as we face our own death.

Death is the most universal human passage outside of birth. It will be the last journey we take, but the one we usually talk least about. Every one of us must face it with some fear, some trembling, some faith and some hope.

If we have the privilege of teaching our children one last, essential lesson, wouldn't we want to do it?

Ernest Becker's classic book, <u>The Denial of Death,</u> puts it this way. "The idea of death, the fear of it, haunts the human animal like nothing else; it is the mainspring of human activity— activity designed largely to avoid the fatality of death, to overcome it by denying in some way that it is the final destiny for man."[129]

"Everyone has to face death alone but everyone does not have to be alone while facing it."[130]

This final phase of life's journey is too often surrounded by denial. Ernest Becker describes death as the mainspring of human activity. Let's be clear, we will all set sail on the journey of death sooner or later.

There are really two essential questions to face as we contemplate this final journey.

Question number one is: When did we, a frail, limited creature on this earth come to know that life will end?

Question number one brings me back to kneeling by a freshly dug grave behind the machine shed of our family farm. Do I remember the story so clearly because my 5-year-old brain at the time had the pain and sorrow so deeply etched into it? Or, is it because the sad story has been repeated to me by adults as I was growing up? It doesn't matter. The story is true, no matter which be the case.

I am kneeling by that freshly dug grave with my little arms desperately hugging the neck of Lady, the family collie. Lady was the first dog we had after moving to the farm from the "big city." She was my constant companion. To be honest, Lady wasn't so much the family dog as she was <u>MY</u> dog.

I witness the scene in my mind. I am beyond consolation. Through my tears I plead, "Wake up, Lady! Wake up!" For, you see, my parents could not bear to tell their desperate 5-year-old son that Lady was dead, killed by the car driving too fast past our front yard.

My parents were without benefit of college "death and dying" classes. My parents were without benefit of grief counseling skills so prudently given to counselors and clergy. My parents did the only thing they could think of to heal a 5-year-old's broken-hearted grief. They tried to ease his grief and pain by saying, "Lady is asleep." But really? If Lady was asleep, why can't I wake her up? "Wake up, Lady! Wake up!"

And now how could I let go of Lady? How could I, a 5-year-old blinded with grief, turn loose the furry softness of Lady's broken neck? "Wake up, Lady! Wake up!" And now the greatest insult of all. Lady, in the ground, never to be seen again. "Wake up, Lady! Wake up!"

When did we, a frail, limited creature on this earth come to know that life will end? For me, it was at that hastily dug grave behind the old machine shed.

Question number two is: When did we, a frail, limited creature on this earth come to know that MY life will end? When did it really sink in that death not only happened to other people and animals, but death would also happen to me? For some that is a difficult question to answer--for others it is easy. For some it happened early on--for others it still has not sunk in.

For me, I suppose the reality of my own death came about due to the whispers coming from the hallway outside my bedroom. I can't tell you exactly how old I was at the time. I can't even tell you why I was so sick. All I know is that the family doctor was called to my bedside. He was the only doctor in our small town. He was called to our farm house to examine me and to offer treatment.

The whispers out in the hallway are what did it. They broke through the denial all humans inherit. I became conscious of the potentially grave consequences of being sick. I had a younger cousin who died of leukemia at a very early age. If my little cousin could be taken from this life, so could I.

The good news is that I survived that childhood sickness. However, I will never outlive the whispers or the fear I saw in the faces of my parents that day.

When did we, a frail, limited creature on this earth come to know that MY life will end? For me it was the day the country doctor whispered in the hallway of our farm house.

The final journey we take in this world will be our own death. The older I get, the more often I think of that journey. It is a journey we must all face. As I said earlier, everyone has to face death alone but everyone does not have to be alone while facing it. I have no clue whether my death will be sooner or later. I have no clue if my death will be prolonged or quick. I do hope that I can face that final journey with dignity, peace and hope. I also hope that I will have one or two loved ones beside me when I make that final journey.

If I have the privilege of teaching my children through my own death, what would the lesson plan look like? Would there be some timeless truths I could live out in those last days? I would like the lesson plan to include three essential ingredients. These three are faith, hope and peace.

FAITH
In the face of death, I would want to spend time remembering the parts of my life that will outlast my body. I would want to remember the people I had the privilege to help, the beautiful places I had the privilege to see and my faith that will outlast not only my generation but countless generations to come.

In the face of death I think I would take out the file in my office labeled "the good stuff." I would read again all the thank you notes I have been blessed by. Maybe this is what is meant by, "Do not lay up for yourselves treasures on earth, where moth and rust consume and where thieves break in and steal, but lay up for yourselves treasure in heaven, where neither moth nor rust consumes and where thieves do not break in and steal. For where your treasure is, there will your heart be also."[131]

As I sail into the final sunset of my life, I hope I can do it with a song in my heart, holy words on my tongue and loved ones by my side. A favorite hymn that I have memorized for a daily bedtime prayer is, "All Praise to Thee, My God, This Night." Embedded in the words of this hymn are the truths of my faith, distilled over many centuries. The words are…

All praise to Thee, my God, this night
for all the blessings of the light.
Keep me, oh keep me, King of kings,
beneath thine own almighty wings.

Forgive me, Lord, for thy dear Son,
the ill that I this day have done;
that with the world, myself, and thee,
I, ere I sleep, at peace may be.

Teach me to live, that I may dread
the grave as little as my bed.
Teach me to die, that so I may
rise glorious at the awesome day.

Oh, may my soul in thee repose,
and may sweet sleep mine eyelids close,
sleep that shall me more vig'rous make,
to serve my God when I awake!

Praise God, from whom all blessings flow;
praise God, all creatures here below;
praise God above, ye heav'nly host;
Praise Father, Son, and Holy Ghost. [132]

HOPE

When my ship sets sail on that last journey I would like to sail away with a sense of hope. I have been at the bedside of many dying people. As they approached death, I would share my primary image of life after death. That image is one where a huge banquet hall is filled with people. God is the host at that banquet. At that banquet there is no more pain, no more scarcity, and no more troubles. Eternal life is a celebration.

After sharing this image with my dying friends I would make a small request. Here is what I would ask. "Would you do me a favor when you get to that great banquet? Would you save a seat for me?" They would always say yes.

Martin Luther said this about death. "If we only knew what joys awaited us in the heavenly kingdom, we would all die of homesickness."

One of my seminary professors once said, "In death, ultimately and finally we are in the hands of God and more than that we just can't say." Pretty good hands to be in I'd say.

After spending years preaching and counseling the bereaved, my image of heaven is still a large banquet hall. Now the only difference in the image I carry with me is the fact that I will have a lot of friends waving for me to come and sit next to them. They have saved a seat for me, fulfilling the promise of Jesus. "I go to prepare a place for you."[133]

PEACE

When my ship sets sail on that last journey, I would like to sail away with a sense of peace.

John Claypool, theologian and author summarizes it best, "Death will make generous givers of us all."

The Bible story that is most haunting to me is from Luke Chapter 12. If you read the story you will understand what Mark Twain meant when he said, "It ain't those parts of the Bible that I can't understand that bother me, it's the parts that I do understand."[134]

One day Jesus responded to a man having a dispute over an inheritance with his brother. Rather than being pulled into the family fight over inheritance money, Jesus tells a story. The story describes a rich fool who has the good problem of having way more grain than he can possibly store in his barns. What does the rich fool do? Does the rich fool considering sharing his excess? Does he rent storage space in the barns of his neighbors? No, the rich fool decides to destroy his old barns and build larger ones.

In the story, God's response to the rich fool's actions is both swift and jarring,

"God said to him, 'Fool! This night your soul is required of you; and the things you have prepared, whose will they be?' So is he who lays up treasure for himself, and is not rich toward God."[135]

As I said, this story has always haunted me by its tragedy and irony. Here is someone who "had it all, yet kept nothing." The rich fool's prudence and planning are mocked by his untimely death.

The words of Frederick Buechner turn this tragic story into grace filled good news.

"The trouble with being rich is that since you can solve with your checkbook virtually all of the practical problems that bedevil ordinary people, you are left with nothing but the great human problems to contend with: how to be happy, how to love and be loved, how to find meaning and purpose in your life.

In desperation, the rich are continually tempted to believe that they can solve these problems too with their checkbook, which is presumably what led Jesus to remark one day that for a rich man to get to Heaven is about as easy as for a Cadillac to get through a revolving door."[136]

When my financial affairs are put in order, I pray that God will have a more generous name for me than "fool." I look forward to leaving this life with a sense of peace because I both received and gave love, because I made a difference with my life by touching the lives of others and because I left this earth a little better than I found it.

So, we have come full circle. This is the point at which Chapter 1, "never work for money or power" and Chapter 7, "a ship in the harbor is safe" connect together. To have a life that is truly full and rich is to have loved and been loved and to have lived with purpose and meaning.

It's a pretty simple formula really. Living rich and full is a matter of… "JUST PLAIN SENSE."

QUESTIONS FOR REFLECTION

1. Have you ever wondered what life would have been like had you taken a different path?
2. Do you ever feel regret over a path you have taken?
3. Name a time when you had the clearest idea of which of two or more paths to take?
4. Have you ever looked back on trials or challenges and come to understand that you were being prepared for something all along?
5. Looking back, has adversity ever prepared you for another chapter of your life?
6. What is the most fun you have ever had without going to jail?
7. When did the reality of death enter your consciousness?
8. When did the reality of YOUR OWN death enter your consciousness?
9. If you could choose, which loved ones would you want around your death bed?
10. Do you have a will, a living will and a durable power of attorney for finances & health care?
11. Have you discussed funeral or memorial wishes with a loved one?
12. What would you like to be remembered for at your death?
13. What is your definition of a life well lived?

Postscript

In any book there are always things left unsaid, truths unrevealed, storys untold. One of the burdens of writing is that there is more to be said but you fear that you may have already said way too much.

So, it will have to end here. If the writing has merit perhaps there will be other stories to be told. Others might notice and offer suggestions on future topics. If it ends at this, then let it be enough.

If I had one goal in this whole endeavor, it was to write a book on truths that I most deeply hold. To that end, my children might understand better the life, values and decisions of their father. All else that may happen with the book is just frosting on the cake.

Endnotes

[1]   Marian Wright Edelman (1939-) President of the Children's Defense Fund, author of <u>The Measure of Success: A Letter to My Children and Yours,</u> copyright May 1, 1992 by Beacon Press, Boston, Massachusetts. Lesson # 4 of "Lessons for Life", page 40.

[2]   Marian Wright Edelman (1939-) President of the Children's Defense Fund, author of <u>The Measure of Success: A Letter to My Children and Yours,</u> copyright May 1, 1992 by Beacon Press, Boston, Massachusetts. Lesson # 4 of "Lessons for Life", page 40.

[3]   I Timothy 6:6-8, RSV

[4]   Epictetus. 55-135 C.E., Greek speaking stoic philosopher.

[5]   <u>Enough: True Measures of Money, Business, and Life,</u> written by John C. Bogle, copyright 2009 by John Wiley & Sons, Inc., Hoboken, New Jersey. page 1

[6]   Matthew 6:19-21, RSV

[7]   Matthew 6:25, RSV

[8]   Josh Billings (1818-1885) American humorist

[9] Mark 9:35, RSV

[10] For details on the conduct of a clearness committee, see Rachel Livsey and Parker J. Palmer, The Courage to Teach: A Guide for Reflection and Renewal copyright 1998, 2007, by John Wiley & sons, pp.43-48.

[11] Let Your Life Speak: Listening for the Voice of Vocation by Parker Palmer, copyright 2,000 by John Wiley & sons, Inc., pages 44-46.

[12] Frederick Buechner, Wishful Thinking: A Theological ABC, Copyright 1973 by Harper & Row, page # 95, the definition of vocation.

[13] Wikipedia, description of the Osprey.

[14] Mark 1:32-35, RSV

[15] Mark 1:33, RSV

[16] A story about the importance of sharpening the ax. Source unknown.

[17] Robert Neale, In Praise of Play (New York:Harper & Row, 1970), pg. 36.

[18] From "Installation of a Pastor", A Companion to Lutheran Book of Worship, pg. 225.

[19] Matthew 6:28-29, RSV

[20] Confession of a Workaholic, copyright 1971 by Wayne E. Oates, Reprinted by permission of the World Publishing Company. Published by G. W. Hall for Abington Festival edition published May, 1978. Quote taken from page 7.

[21] Attributed to Arnold Zach, lawyer/friend of the late Senator Paul Tsongas of Massachusetts (1941-1997).

[22] "Pastor Ingqvist's Trip to Orlando" by Garrison Keillor. From *Gospel Birds* published by HighBridge Audio, copyright 1985 Garrison Keillor (P) 1985 Minnesota Public Radio

[23] The Will Rogers Book, copyright 1972 by Paula McSpadden Love, a niece of Will Rogers's, curator of The Will Rogers Memorial in Claremore, Oklahoma, pg. 166 & 167.

[24] Karl Paul Reinhold Niebuhr 1892 – 1971, American theologian.

[25] Attributed to H. Jackson Brown, Jr.

[26] Depression is Contagious, copyright 2009 by Michael D. Yapko, Ph.D., by Free Press, page 53.

[27] Ibid, Page 91.

[28] Generation to Generation copyright 1985 by Edwin H. Friedman, The Guilford Press, page 27.

[29] Ibid, page 39.

[30] Listen, author anonymous, poem reprinted from ACCORD Magazine.

[31] Psalm 56:3, NASB

[32] From "Make It Simple" a stewardship resource produced by The Evangelical Lutheran Church in America, "That Ten Percent Thing" featuring Barb Debski.

[33] Attributed to Helen Keller, (1880-1968) Educator, journalist & co-founder of ACLU.

[34] Pastor Rick Warren, The Purpose Driven Life: What on Earth Am I Here For?, 2002, Zondervan Publishing. Chapter 3, page 32

[35] For the complete poem, The Station, written by Robert J. Hastings go to robertjhastings.net

[36] From Forest E. Witcraft, (1894-1967) scholar, teacher and scout leader.

[37] Ibid

[38] Uncertain origin (Alexander Hamilton, Peter Marshall, Ginger Rogers, Malcolm X)

[39] William James (1842-1910) American philosopher & psychologist.

[40] Giving to God by Mark Allan Powell, Copyright 2006 by Wm. B. Eerdmans Publishing Co. Grand Rapids, Michigan. Page 108

[41] Parables of Peanuts by Robert Short. Copyright 1968 by Harper & Row, Publishers, New York, NY.

[42] Lewis Carroll (1832-1898) Alice in Wonderland, written by English logician, mathematician, photographer, novelist.

[43] Jean Paul Getty (1892-1976) Industrialist, founder of Getty Oil Company.

[44] A eulogy about Ray Kaczmarek given by Pastor Tom Sublett, February 3, 2008.

⁴⁵   Henry Brooks Adams (1838-1918) American writer.

⁴⁶   Attributed to O.A. Battista or M. Grundler.

⁴⁷   "Who Gets All the Good Stuff", <u>Modern Maturity Magazine,</u> June/ July 2001, written by Dr. Terry D. Hargrave, Associate Professor of Counseling at West Texas A & M University.

⁴⁸   <u>The Measure of a Man A Spiritual Autobiography</u> by Sidney Poitier. Copyright, 2000 HarperCollins Publishers Inc., NY, NY. Page 66.

⁴⁹   John Wooden (1910-2010) basketball coach.

⁵⁰   Quote of uncertain origin.

⁵¹   Redd Foxx (1922-1991) comedian, actor.

⁵²   <u>Wishful Thinking </u>by Frederick Buechner, copyright, 1973 Harper & Row, Publishers, page 95.

⁵³   <u>The Divine Drama-Our Narrative</u> page 155, by Harry Wendt, Crossways International, 1993 Minneapolis, MN.

⁵⁴   Bob Connolly, financial consultant for "The James Company", Milwaukee, Wisconsin.

⁵⁵   To research more facts about the world's population go to the internet and search: "If the world were only 100 people." You'll be amazed.

⁵⁶   From the Last Will and Testament of Jack & Kathleen Ottoson.

[57]   Attributed to Peter Simmel.

[58]   See Wikipedia, Stanford Marshmallow Experiment, 1972, by psychologist Walter Mischel of Stanford University.

[59]   Benjamin Franklin (1706-1790) Author, printer, diplomat, inventor, satirist.

[60]   Attributed to Arnold Zach, lawyer friend of the late Senator Paul Tsongas of Massachusetts

[61]   Anonymous

[62]   Congratulatory notes from Terra J. Brock and Nathan D. Ottoson.

[63]   James Arthur Baldwin, American Essayist, Playwright and Novelist (1924-1987)

[64]   Ibid

[65]   Samuel Langhorne Clemens (Mark Twain) 11/30/1835-4/21/1910 American author/humorist.

[66]   Pastor Rick Warren, The Purpose Driven Life: What on Earth am I here for?, 2002, Zondervan Publishing. Chapter 3, page 32

[67]   The Road Less Traveled, M. Scott Peck, Simon & Schuster, 1978 page 63.

[68]   The Road Less Traveled, M. Scott Peck, Simon & Schuster, 1978 page 31.

69   www.aa.org/assets/en_ug/smf-121_en.pdf

70   www.articlesbase.com, "The facts about drug abuse prevention."

71   The Story of Psychology chapter on The Social Psychologists, "Attribution Theory" page 427.

72   Exodus Counseling Center, "Journey Notes", fall 1992.

73   William James (1842-1910) American psychologist/philosopher.

74   Charles Swindoll (1934-) evangelical Christian pastor, author, educator.

75   Anonymous.

76   Og Mandino (1923-1996) American author of The Greatest Salesman in the World.

77   Abraham Lincoln (1809-1865) 16th President of the United States.

78   Clinical Pastoral Education Journal, September 10, 1979, Jack Ottoson and Fr. Mike Mack.

79   By Bad Habits t-shirts. Search internet for sources.

80   Author Unknown

81   Dan Thompson, history teacher, Pecatonica High School, Pecatonica, Illinois.

82   H.L. Menken, (1880-1956) journalist, essayist & satirist.

83   The Road Less Traveled, M. Scott Peck, Simon & Schuster, 1978 pages 51-54.

84   Unknown origin.

85   Unknown Origin

86   Marlene Dietrich 1901-1992, German-American actress & singer.

87   Father Bernard Cooke, S.J., Loyola University, Professor of Theology Emeritus.

88   Lake Wobeggone Days copyright 1985 by Garrison Keillor, Penguin Group.

89   www.pbs.org People & Discoveries, Dr. Sigmund Freud, (1856-1939), Austrian neurologist who founded the discipline of psychoanalysis.

90   Unknown origin

91   Bruce W. Thielmann, (1933-1994) Pastor of 1st Presbyterian Church, Pittsburgh, PA. As quoted in The Wittenburg Door – No. 36 April-May 1977.

92   See http://growdeep.blogspot.com/2010/04/pulpit-calls.html.

93   Pastor Loci Column, "Staying the Hammers", Lutheran Partners Magazine, January/February 1995, pg. 28, written by Pastor Steven L. McKinley.

94   Ibid

95   Herman Hesse, 1877-1962, German novelist.

96   John Powell, <u>Why am I afraid to tell you who I am?</u> Copyright 1969, by Argus Communications, page 111.

97   William Shakespeare, 1564-1616, English poet & playwright. From ThinkExist.com & GoodReads.com. There is debate about these words as authentic Shakespeare.

98   Frederick Buechner, <u>Wishful Thinking: A Theological ABC,</u> Copyright 1973 by Harper & Row, page # 54, the definition of love.

99   It is important to note here that the New Testament uses at least four words that we might translate "love." The Greek word "agape", used in this command from Matthew 19:19, is described as "divine, unconditional, self-sacrificing, active, volitional and thoughtful love." (Wikipedia).

100   John 15:17, RSV.

101   Story heard on radio Z 88.3, a central Florida radio channel.

102   A phrase coined by Dr. Martin Luther (1483-1546), German monk, priest, Dr. of Theology and iconic figure of the Protestant Reformation. In the Smalcald Articles, Luther explains, "The first and chief article is this: Jesus Christ, our God and Lord, died for our sins and was raised again for our justification. (Romans 3:24-25).

103   Oscar Wilde, Irish Poet, Novelist, Dramatist, Critic. 1854-1900.

104   Matthew 5:48, RSV.

[105] Copyright, 2009 by the *Christian Century*, "You, therefore, must be perfect", Fred B. Craddock, is reprinted by permission from the February 7-14, 1990 issue of the *Christian Century*, www.christiancentury.org

[106] October 1975 interview of Dr. Joseph Sittler, (1904-1987) American Lutheran theologian & professor at The Divinity School of the University of Chicago and Lutheran School of Theology at Chicago.

[107] From the wedding vows written by Jack and Kathy Ottoson and exchanged on December 16, 1972.

[108] October 1975 interview of Dr. Joseph Sittler, (1904-1987) American Lutheran theologian & professor at The Divinity School of the University of Chicago, Lutheran School of Theology at Chicago.

[109] Attributed to many persons...William Shedd -19th Century Theologian, John A. Shedd–author, Salt From my Attic (1928), Benazir Bhutto, Grant M. Bright, Rear Admiral-Grace Murray Hooper. Researched at: forum.quoteland.com

[110] Ibid

[111] Woody Allen (1935-) American actor, author, screenwriter and film maker.

[112] Richard Halverson, Chaplain-U.S. Senate, Presbyterian, appointed February 2, 1981.

[113] Taken from "Thoughts in Solitude" by Thomas Merton, a Cistercian Monk, Abbey of Gethsemane, Bardstown, Kentucky

[114] Abraham Lincoln (1809-1865) 16th President of the United States.

[115] Millard Fuller, CEO of Habitat for Humanity.

[116] Pastor Rick Warren, The Purpose Driven Life: What on Earth am I here for?, 2002, Zondervan Publishing. Chapter 3, page 34

[117] Frederick Buechner, Wishful Thinking A Theological ABC, Copyright 1973 by Harper & Row, page 95, the definition of vocation.

[118] For an excellent article on Adversity Quotients (AQ) and ministry, see Lutheran Partners magazine, November/December 2000. "Recognizing and Lifting One's AQ" by Pastor Steven L. McKinley. McKinley refers to the work of Edward O. Welles and Paul Stoltz in the July 2000 issue of Inc. magazine.

[119] Confucius, (551-447 BCE) Chinese teacher, editor, politician, philosopher

[120] Taken from Balancing Heaven and Earth by Robert Johnson, copyright 1998 by HarperCollins Publishers.

[121] Matthew 25:40, RSV.

[122] Alice Anne Connor, writer for Kenosha News, Saturday June 22, 1996

[123] Clinical Pastoral Education Journal, September 10, 1979, Jack Ottoson and Fr. Mike Mack.

[124] Letter in autumn of 1996 from Bob & Audrey sending a generous check (with $.70 added for good measure)

[125] Gary Player, (November 1, 1935-) South African golfer who has won 165 tournaments, on 6 continents, over 6 decades of play.

[126] Jeremiah 29:11, RSV

[127] Interview: Kathleen Turner, <u>Arthritis Today</u> magazine, December 2002, page 44.

[128] Sean Rouse, of Houston, Texas, rheumatoid arthritis patient.

[129] Ernest Becker, <u>The Denial of Death,</u> Copyright 1973 by The Free Press, from preface page 1.

[130] Middle of the night insight, Jack Ottoson, April 5, 2013

[131] Matthew 6:19-21, RSV.

[132] TALLIS CANON, Text: Thomas Ken (1637-1711). Tune: Thomas Tallis(1505-1585)

[133] John 14:2, RSV.

[134] Samuel Langhorne Clemens (Mark Twain) 11/30/1835-4/21/1910 American author/humorist.

[135] Luke 12:20-21, RSV.

[136] Frederick Buechner, <u>Wishful Thinking A Theological ABC,</u> Copyright 1973 by Harper & Row, page 81, the definition of rich.

CPSIA information can be obtained at www.ICGtesting.com
Printed in the USA
LVOW11s2326130416

483512LV00002B/2/P